-2007-

To Judy

Many happy days

of quilting!

Love,

Ann Bernius

AROUND THE QUILT FRAME

STORIES AND MUSINGS
ON THE QUILTER'S CRAFT

Edited by Kari Cornell
Voyageur Press

First published in 2006 by Voyageur Press, an imprint of MBI Publishing
Company, Galtier Plaza, Suite 200, 380 Jackson Street, St. Paul, MN
55101-3885 USA.

MBI titles are also available at discounts in bulk quantity for industrial
or sales-promotional use. For details write to Special Sales Manager at
MBI Publishing Company, Galtier Plaza, Suite 200, 380 Jackson Street,
St. Paul, MN 55101-3885 USA.

ISBN-13: 978-0-7603-2537-7
ISBN-10: 0-7603-2537-5

Editor: Kari Cornell
Jacket Design: Maria Friedrich
Book Design: LeAnn Kuhlmann

Cover Art: top photo © Library of Congress; bottom photo © Tony
O'Brien, quilt used courtesy of the Washington County Historical Society.

Printed in the United States of America

Permissions

Contents

INTRODUCTION

The first time I ever sat around a quilt frame I was ten years old. It was the late 1970s, and my mom was caught up in the back-to-the-earth movement, making as many things as she could by hand. She knotted macramé lamps, plant hangers, and owl wall hangings; sewed most of the clothes my brother and I wore (matching outfits, of course); kept an extensive vegetable garden; and made her own granola. So when it came time to redecorate my room—I had grown tired of the pink walls and ruffled canopy bed—she offered to sew new curtains and make a quilt . . . if I would help her with the design.

Being a typical child of the 1970s, I loved Little House on the Prairie, owned more than one Holly Hobby doll, and couldn't get enough of rainbows and unicorns. It's no surprise, then that I decided we would paint my room yellow and make a quilt decorated with rainbows, hearts, strawberries (in honor of my Strawberry Shortcake doll, of course), and a shining sun. I chose calicos in primary colors and decided on a plain muslin background.

I remember being so excited to actually design my very own quilt, and I took the whole thing very seriously. I sketched out my ideas and handed them over to my mom for execution. The quilt consisted of twelve blocks—a yellow sun with red rays glimmered from the center block, surrounded by the four strawberries. Six rainbows floating on calico blue clouds banked the strawberries, and the hearts anchored the four corners. A rainbow border framed the quilt, and calico sashing, a different color for each row, connected the vibrant blocks.

My mom machine-pieced the blocks, but we did the quilting by hand. One of my mom's friends brought over a quilt frame and we set it up in the family room, in front of the sliding-glass patio doors that overlooked the backyard. For months we held a quilting bee each Sunday, and four or five of my mom's friends would come over to stitch and chat.

Looking back on it, I'm amazed that I was able to sit still for the better part of a Sunday afternoon and quilt. But I loved the time we spent around that frame. It wasn't so much the act of quilting that I relished, because I wasn't very good at it and it seemed to take forever. It was the conversation and the feeling of camaraderie that I looked forward to every Sunday. I never said much myself, but I soaked up stories about the quilters' lives, families, and friends. I was at the age when I wanted more than anything in the world to be grown up, and spending a few hours each week surrounded by women I admired was the next best thing. To me, this time was golden.

The stories collected on the pages of this book are not so different from those I listened to as I added wobbly stitches to my rainbow quilt some twenty-five years ago. Whether it be the humorous musings of Ami Simms in her quest to finish one of the myriad UFOs (unfinished objects) found in every nook and cranny of her house; Lisa Boyer's approach to "organizing" her ever-growing stash of fabric; the warmth of spending time around a quilt frame surrounded by good friends in Sandra Dallas's piece; or the hardships endured by the pioneer quilters who struggled to create adequate coverings for their beds and walls, there's a little something for every quilt lover. I hope you enjoy the book.

Chapter One

TO BE A QUILTER

"I am a quiltmaker, purely and simply put. There is no need to explain that to another quilter. . . . The astonishing satisfaction that comes from quilting is beyond explanation."

—Helen Kelley, Every Quilt Tells a Story, 2003

ENTER THE HOME OF A QUILTER and you immediately know where you are. Surely there's a closet, room, or maybe even an entire floor (one should be so lucky!) dedicated to quilting. A sewing machine stands at the ready on a work table in the corner, the infamous "stash" of fabric bursts from a wall of shelves, the latest project-in-the-works covers all available horizontal space, including the floor, and, where the floor is visible, millions of tiny, tiny threads in all colors of the rainbow lie scattered about like confetti. But these tangible tools and supplies are only part of the picture. In truth, the essence of what it means to be a quilter isn't something you can actually put your finger on. It's the creative spirit, sense of adventure, generosity, and warmth that makes a quilter a quilter. In each of the following essays, the authors talk about what it means to be a quilter, whether it be the many unfinished objects (affectionately known as UFOs) hidden in every corner of the house, or the out-of-control fabric stash and how it should/should not be managed.

FEELING GOOD

by Helen Kelley

Helen Kelley is a quiltmaker, lecturer, author, and instructor based in Minneapolis, Minnesota. Widely respected by the quilting community, Helen has made more than 115 quilts. For the past twenty years, she has written a monthly column in Quilter's Newsletter Magazine. Every Quilt Tells a Story and Helen Kelley's Joy of Quilting, both published by Voyageur Press, collect many of her columns into book form. The special bond between quilters and the characteristics they share—warmth, a sense of humor, and the urge to collect yards and yards of fabric—are a common theme in Helen's articles. In this piece, from Helen Kelley's Joy of Quilting, she struggles to explain the appeal of quilting to a nonquilter . . . not an easy task!

H as anyone ever asked you a question that left you so speechless, so shocked and surprised that you couldn't frame a reply? I was talking to a lady. She was a very nice lady, someone I had never met before. We made light conversation. We asked each other the usual questions, like, "What do you do?"

"I'm a quiltmaker," I told her.

There was a long, uneasy pause as the lady tried to sort this out in her mind. It was as if I had said that I raise barracudas or fly stunt planes. Obviously, making quilts was a new thought to her. She was groping for a polite reply.

"I suppose you have lots of quilts?" she asked.

"Oh, yes, lots of them," I said. "I always have one in the making and one in my head."

There was another uneasy pause. After another silence, she asked, "What do you do with them?"

"I, well, I . . . you know, I . . . I . . ."

What do I do with my quilts? It was as if the lady had asked me what I do with my children. What do I do with my quilts? I told the nice lady something that I thought she could understand. I told her that I have a few on my beds, and that occasionally, I give one of my quilts as a gift. Sometimes, I wrap a grandchild in one for a nap. I may snuggle under one while I watch TV. I may hang one on my wall to delight me each time I pass it. I did not add that I have lots of quilts on my shelves that I count, talk to, and fold and refold. She would not have understood that I like to feel my quilts.

When I make a quilt, I find joy in puzzling out the colors and the design. I love to sort the fabrics, to cut and stack them, to stitch them together so that they lie smooth and flat and the hues melt into each other, piece by piece, until the patterns take shape and bloom. The most pleasure in all those fabrics, though, is that I like the feel of them as I work.

The rhythm of quilting sings to me. It is like a seda-tive, like the gentle rocking of a drifting boat as it nestles in the water. My hands move across the face of the quilt, stitching, tacking down the puffs and the billows, etching the pattern, lifting it into a third dimension. The softness is a silent pleasure. The feel is satisfying.

When I finish my quilt, I lay it out on the bed or hang it high on my wall, and I run my hands across the surface. I smooth it and pat it down. I reassure it. There is a shiver of pleasure that runs through me when I see my quilt finished and soft and gentle and touchable. The nice lady would not have understood all of this.

We, as quilters, gather in guilds each month to meet people who all speak our language and experience the same love. I do not need to explain to each of you that

I love to feel my quilts. You know what I mean. As quilters, we sew a variety of quilts. We may make quilted toaster covers or dog blankets. We may make baby buntings or fashionable vests or draft stoppers for our doors. We may make stuffed bears and rabbits wearing patchwork dresses, or elegant pillows, dormitory comforters, or commodious tote bags. We may make big, soft quilts or small wall hangings. Whatever we make, we all do the same things—sorting, cutting, stitching, and feeling.

A person may read home-decorating magazines or visit antique stores to admire quilts, but until he or she has actually sewn pieces of fabric together and stitched them into a quilt, until that person has touched and felt them, handled them and loved them, that person cannot understand the mystery of quilt-making. Admire them? Oh, certainly. That's easy. Quilts are beautiful to look at, but to be truly loved, quilts have to be felt. Tell me, if you met someone today, someone who asked you what you do with your quilts, how ever would you put your depth of feeling into words?

WHO NEEDS QUILT GUILT?!

by Ami Simms

In the following essay, which originally appeared in the July issue of her electronic newsletter, Ami Simms comes to terms with the guilt she feels over the myriad projects she has scattered throughout the house. Ami Simms is a quilter, lecturer, author, and teacher. She was named 2005 Teacher of the Year by Professional Quilter magazine. Visit her online at www.AmiSimms.com.

I t's July, and 2005 is technically halfway through. That's a disappointing thought because that means I should have at least made a dent in my UFOs. The plan in January was to finish at least some of the sewing projects I started! Yeah right.

Mind you, I'm not complaining. That could require action, like a rededication to my goals, or at least a list of projects I wanted to tackle in some kind of priority ranking that I could check off. I'm just whining.

Whining, as I have taught my husband, is another way of sharing. It may sound like I want him to do something about whatever it is that I'm whining about but, after twenty-eight years of training, he knows he is only supposed to commiserate with me and not try to suggest ways to fix whatever I'm whining about.

Fixing should occur only after suggesting, which is sometimes confused with nagging (but isn't) as in, "Gee, I noticed the drain in the bathtub is really slow." That means I want him to pour some of that glop down the drain to melt the clog. I could just say, "Honey, please fix the drain in the tub," but that smacks of a demand which is like a nag, but altogether different. I certainly don't want to be demanding, so it's up to him to note the subtle difference, and/or read my mind, which apparently he has not done, since the drain has been really slow since May. But I digress. . . .

I decided at the beginning of this year to actually finish something. Anything. Preferably something that has already been in progress for some time, but I was going to settle for finally weaving the ending tails of three knitted scarves that were supposed to be Christmas presents but that have been living on my ironing board because the intended recipients didn't attend the party. I've been moving the scarves from the ironing board to the cutting table and back again since mid-December. Apparently I don't mind, because they are still not finished.

I did finish two pairs of pants for my mother, but the pieces for pair #3 rotate around the room with the scarves. Madison got a homemade tuxedo but Steve's shirt and slacks, requiring a button and hem respectively, have lived in my ironing bin for at least six years. Out of sight; out of mind. Or, maybe in my case, just out of my mind.

I cornered the market last Halloween on collapsible fabric trick-or-treat pumpkins. I bought six of them at the dollar store because I thought for sure they would make great fabric bowls. I took one apart for the pattern, and used fish fabric to make a . . . wait for it . . . fish bowl. Another twelve minutes with a needle and thread and I could be done with it. I'm waiting for it to morph into something worthy of twelve minutes of my time, so it sits on the edge of my sewing-machine table and periodically gets knocked off into the garbage bucket below. I fish it out and put it back on the table. I think it's trying tell me something. If I let it stay in the trash, perhaps I won't have to finish it.

Jennie received two quilts when she graduated from high school. The first was a photo-transfer quilt which lives on her bed at school. The second quilt she had to give back because it needed about twenty hours of machine quilting for completion. And it still does. She graduates from college in April 2006, so I figure I'm OK. If not, she's planning on graduate school. With any luck she'll go for her Ph.D.

The Big Green Monster Quilt needs about thirty hours of quilting and she too will be done. I was appliquéing the pieces for that before the turn of the century. I finally started quilting in 2001 and haven't taken a stitch since. It lives in a plastic laundry basket that gets kicked from the sewing room to the living room and back again. I refold it from time to time, but that's all the action it gets.

I've got another giant quilt made of some of Mom's hand-dye-stamped fabrics puzzled together. It's basted and ready to go. I can't remember what that looks like it's been so long. Stacked neatly nearby are no less than nine tops ranging in age from "Pieced-Before-We-Moved" (pre-1989) to Just-Completed. I'm waiting for them to decide how they want to be quilted and to mark themselves.

At least twenty-four containers hold projects that have blocks assembled, along with matching fabric, and in some cases a pattern to follow. Another half a dozen containers hold designs, sketches for quilts whose parts haven't yet materialized. I also have three pizza boxes filled with 2-inch orange, green, and purple squares that were going to be something very important, I just can't remember what. Under them are about 4,000 half-square triangles leftover from an Ocean Waves frenzy that spawned one finished quilt, one top, and plans for several more, the pieces for which have been curing for over a decade.

And that's not counting the basement. Or the nonrecreational projects I want to develop into books, patterns, and workshops.

It's not like I've quit sewing. When I do have time—on airplanes, in hotel rooms—and when I can pry myself away from the computer at home and sit with my family and veg out in front of TV, I reach for my invisibly appliquéd Midget Double Wedding Ring pieces. I've made enough "melons" to take it from wall-hanging to couch-potato cover. It may hit bed size any time now. Because I keep buying more fabric for it, I can't sew the melons together yet unless I want a visual timeline of my fabric purchases, so I'm waiting until the new get fully integrated with the old. I have purchased enough fat quarters and skinny minis for a king-size quilt. I'm just hoping it won't come to that.

So why don't I finish more things? To be sure, I lose interest in some projects, like the fourteenth Twisted Sisters quilt. Great pattern, but I've already moved on. Some projects had little merit to begin with and got farther along than they had a right to. Amish Center Pizza is probably a case in point. I'll probably never get to that one. Technical difficulties pose a problem with some projects. After I stitched twenty-four folded pineapple blocks, I realized that all the extra fabric in the folds will require me to steam-roller the seams if they are ever to lay flat. Self doubt and faltering inspiration is to blame for tops waiting to be quilted. How shall I quilt them? What motif will transport the work to a higher level? Indecision rears its ugly head more often than I care to admit. Let's say I've got thirty minutes. What do I want to sew on? I just can't make up my mind! With so many choices (even if I can't remember all the projects I could pick from), I give up and fold laundry instead.

Finally, I'm my own worst enemy. I have never been able to accurately estimate the amount of time anything will take. Optimism takes hold and I jump in with both feet, regardless. Like last week's new project of making little memory quilts from my mother-in-law's shirts for all six of her children. In nine days. I just realized today I'm not going to make it! They'll have to wait for Christmas—if they're lucky.

So does it all matter in the end? No. I don't really care if my UFOs sit for another year. I live for thrills. I love the way my brain tingles when I get a new idea, collect the fabric, and solve the puzzle of how to create it. That's where the buzz is! I've decided to let it be irrelevant if the project is ever completed. Who needs the guilt? Thanks for letting me whine. I feel better already.

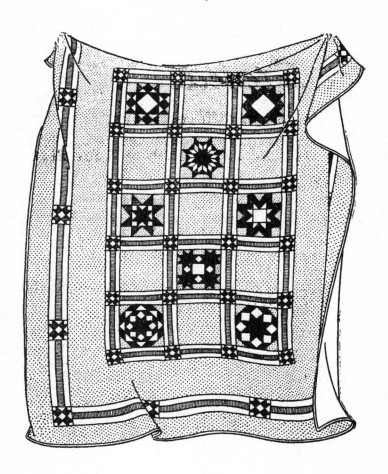

A GREAT QUILTING TRUTH OF THE UNIVERSE

by Lisa Boyer

Most quilters keep some sort of a fabric stash, comprised of remnants left over from previous projects, or a yard or two in an irresistible pattern bought on a whim at the last quilt show. But is it orderly? In "A Great Quilting Truth of the Universe," quilter Lisa Boyer is put on the spot when her sister calls to ask how she organizes her stash. Lisa designs patterns, teaches quilt classes, and writes about the Hawaiian Island of Kaua'i, where she lives with her husband and son. This essay originally appeared in That Dorky Homemade Look: Quilting Lessons from a Parallel Universe, which was published by Good Books in 2002.

M y sister called me long distance from her workplace between patients today. She had a pressing question that had been causing her to lose sleep. She wanted to know how I organize my fabric stash. As an avid beginner, she told me that she first had her small fabric collection organized into lights and darks, but now her stash had grown, and that system of organization was simply not sufficient anymore.

She asked me if I arranged my fabric collection by color wheel, you know, colors and their analogous counterparts on one shelf, complementary colors on the other. Or did I arrange the fabrics by cool colors versus warm colors? Or perhaps according to scale of print: separate stacks for large florals, small geometrics, and blenders? And how did I catalog amounts? Make tags? Keep a fabric journal?

As the experienced quilter in the family, I quickly tried to make up an answer. "Oh . . . yes . . . all those things work . . . ," I stammered, daunted by her enthusiasm. I was glad at that point that she lived at the other end of California and couldn't see into my sewing room at that moment. "And don't forget to separate out the monochromatics from the polychromatics," I reminded her, not having the slightest idea what I meant.

After we hung up, a great Quilting Truth of the Universe suddenly came to me. (If nine more come to me, I promise to travel to the nearest mountaintop and write them all down on stone tablets.) This great Quilting Truth of the Universe is a simple one: each person has her (or his) own precious quilting personality which permeates every aspect of her (or his) art, from organization to execution to exhibition. And because each of us is unique, each quilt is beautifully and wondrously different. It's as if our souls were laid open and squashed down into every color and fiber of the thing. A quilt is a song, a dance, a soft soothing poem, or a tumultuous scream of panic. (Okay, maybe I am the only one who has ever made a tumultuous-scream-of-panic-quilt, but you get the idea.)

Yes, yes, yes, I know you have heard this all before, that each quilt is unique and individual, blah, blah, blah. I have, too. But do you really cherish your own quilting style? Do you love your own work, no matter what your mistakes are? Do you realize that your quilts symbolize the very essence of your personality? Can you look at your own quilting mistakes, regrets, misjudgments, and shortcomings, and give yourself permission to be proud of yourself? Can you look at yourself in the form of a quilt?

My sister and I are vastly different illustrations of the above truth. She conceives in her mind the exact quilt she would like to make, carefully selects fabric from the quilting shop, takes her choices home, and neatly folds, catalogs, and arranges her selections according to the color wheel. She then uses it as planned in a carefully executed color study. Her quilts show that she is creative, colorful, imaginative, and . . . well, beautiful.

On the other hand, let me tell you what happens to me. Since I am constantly on a budget, I can never afford more than a half-yard of anything. I go to the quilt shop and try to cover my ears and use my eyes only. I look at all the gorgeous fabric parading before me, like contestants at the Miss Universe Pageant. But the same thing always happens to me. It comes on slowly at first, somewhat subliminally, but it creeps slowly into my consciousness . . . there . . . did you hear that? A whimper? A tiny little plaintive cry emanating from the homely bolt at the back of the store? "Buy me and make me beautiful!" it cries. "Love me . . . nobody else will! If you don't buy me, I'll end up on the sale rack and be puckered and scrunched up forever in a . . . gasp! . . . rag rug! Save meeeeee!"

"No!" I yell back. "Pick on someone else! I saved all your ugly brothers and sisters! Leave me alone!"

"Appreciate me! Showcase me! Make me into a quilt!" it whines pitifully.

I never win this fight, though. I own the Humane Society of Fabric. And with all that, you'd think that the fabric would be grateful. But it isn't. Once I get it home and put it on the shelf with the other fabrics, they all wait until I am out of the room. Then they prowl and roam like beasts. They tear big pieces out of each other. They mate and create little genetic mutants of fabric that I swear I didn't buy. Worst of all, when I try to use them in a quilt, they get really ugly. They conspire to vibrate and glow and wander all over the place, losing their little points in the process.

And this is precisely what fascinates me about quilting. If I could control and tame the fabrics, I think I might get bored. But the fabrics continue to surprise and thrill me. They have their own personalities. They leap and contort and complain, and somehow I talk them down and settle them into a quilt. My mistakes are most often better than my best-laid plans.

But I didn't tell any of this to my sister. Her life is as well planned and structured as her gorgeous quilts are, and the organization of her stash will be another aspect of her quilting style that makes her unique.

And frankly, she thinks I'm weird enough without having to hear that fabric talks to me. I won't tell her that I wrap myself up in my own artwork and giggle out loud, pleased as punch in what I have created. But I'll bet you anything that she does exactly the same thing.

WHAT WILL WE THINK OF NEXT?

by Ami Simms

There's definitely something about doing it the old-fashioned way that conjures up fond memories. In the following essay, Ami Simms takes a trip down memory lane, remembering the peacefulness of handquilting at the quilt frame, the distinct sound the scissors made as her mother cut fabric on the dining room table, and drawing quilt designs on graph paper with a just-sharpened pencil. At the same time, she takes stock in the modern tools that make quilting a breeze. Think about it: where would we be today without rotary cutters and computers?

M y mother used to make all my clothes when I was growing up. She'd clear off the dining room table after supper, spread out the fabric, and pin the pattern pieces to it. Then she'd use the big heavy shears to cut out each piece. I'll never forget that sound as the scissors resonated against the wood: deep and solid. Those scissors meant business. Go ahead, grab your Ginghers and a piece of cotton, run over to the dining room table, and make a few cuts. Isn't that wonderful?

Quilters hardly use scissors anymore. We're all about rotary cutting. Sure, it's faster and more accurate, but every once in a while we should cut something "by hand." Just for the sound.

I remember designing my first quilts on graph paper. That was way before I got my first computer, the one with the 6-inch floppy disks. (One "floppy" had the word-processing program on it; the other was for data.) Graph paper was pretty magical way back then. Sketching a few squares and triangles with a sharp pencil unlocked the mystery of just how the block would go together.

I liked the smell of a freshly sharpened pencil. I'd always sharpen more pencils than I needed. I wasn't crazy about blackening the side of my hand with smeared lead (it's a left-handed thing) or having the very tip break off if I pushed too hard. But, the sound of the pencil on the paper was good. The best was being able to outline each patch so my lines were exactly on their lines. No wobbles; no strays. The pencil lines were straight and dark. Then I'd finish off the Master Plan by filling in all the boxes with colored pencils. I'd staple a little swatch at the bottom and make a "key" so I'd know which patch was what color. Never mind that we were only allowed to use three fabrics back then: a print and two coordinating solids. There was comfort in graph paper.

Now everybody designs on the computer. Electric Quilt can spit out perfect renderings and even calculates yardage. Your hands don't even get dirty. I found one of my graph-paper patterns the other day, with the colored pencil and the swatches. It was impressive. I think I'll frame it.

When I started quilting, everybody handquilted. They were pretty snotty about it if you wanted to machine quilt. Machine quilting was almost as evil as running down Main Street without any clothes on.

I handquilted all my quilts and it took a long time, and I enjoyed it. I got good enough to get fourteen stitches to an inch and hardly ever bled. I loved the feel of the thread in my hands and reveled in the little hills and valleys my needle made. I petted them constantly. I liked the sound the thread made as I pulled it through the fabric and I found immense satisfaction in pulling that thread just enough but not too much. Sewing by hand freed my mind to wander. The repetition was relaxing. It fed my soul.

Most everybody machine quilts now. So do I. I can hardly find the time to quilt at all, so I'm grateful that when I do sit down I can get a lot done. Getting in the groove of a free-motion motif is an absolute gas, and filling up a quilt with lots of quilting is very satisfying. I pulled out a handquilting project a few weeks ago and have been quilting for a few hours every evening since then. All those good feelings came right back. I guess it's a lot like riding a bicycle—you don't ever forget. I think I'm going to make more time for it.

Things have changed over the years. It's been nearly thirty years since I first picked up a quilting needle, which is impossible because I'm not that old yet. Things have changed mostly for the better. I'm not giving up my rotary cutter any time soon. I'm a much better quilt designer with a mouse than I ever was with a pencil. With all the quilts I want to make I'd be nuts to stop machine quilting. Still, it's nice to use my "rear view mirror" every now and again to revisit my past. Having a history is good. It gives you options. What a happy discovery!

Chapter Two

THE QUILT SHOW
AND BEYOND

"My first quilt show was a real eye-opener. . . .
The instant we walked into the show I knew we
were out of our league. In fact, we weren't even
playing the same game. We loved every quilt we
saw and couldn't for the life of us figure out why
they all weren't wearing ribbons."

—Ami Simms, How <u>Not</u> to Make a Prize-Winning Quilt, 1994

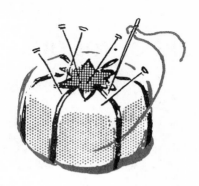

IF THE QUILT SHOP IS THE QUILTMAKER'S candy store, the quilt show is seventh heaven. At some of the larger shows, attendees gawk at hundreds of new and old quilts on display, test out the latest high-tech gadget, or take a class to learn a new technique. Of course, one of the main attractions at any show is the shopping. Shop owners come from all over to sell anything and everything related to quilting: vintage quilts, fat quarters in happy reproduction feed-sack prints, patterns, books, Olfa mats and rotary cutters, thread in every color imaginable, you name it. And quilters come ready to buy, many toting along carry-on bags with wheels to haul home their purchases. But most importantly, quilters attend quilt shows to connect with like-minded souls and to celebrate a pastime they love. The essays in this chapter touch on everything from the lure of the quilt show, to the quilter's quest for the ultimate quilt or yard of fabric, to the kindred spirits they meet along the way.

THE LURE OF THE QUILT SHOW

by Jean Ray Laury

People go to quilt shows for a variety of reasons. Many seek inspiration, which the quilts on display are quick to provide. Others go to shop or take a class with a favorite instructor. But as Jean Ray Laury points out in the following essay, most go to recharge and connect with friends in the quilting community. Jean's lifetime of work in quilting has been varied and exciting. She has written more than a dozen books, including Imagery on Fabric, The Photo Transfer Handbook, and The Getting It All Together Handbook. She has lectured and taught worldwide, from Japan to Norway, and Australia to South Africa. She is currently designing fabrics for Free Spirit and preparing for a major exhibition at the San Jose Museum of Quilts.

Several years ago I headed off on my magic carpet—in this case a quilt. I was traveling, eagerly, from the West Coast to the East.

When I boarded the plane, the gentleman in line behind me took a seat beside me. We exchanged the usual pleasantries, and then I sank into my seat, ready for a good read. My seatmate tucked his gold-monogrammed briefcase under the seat and smoothed down his elegant pinstriped suit. I couldn't resist glancing down to see if I had loose quilting threads dangling from my clothes.

He suddenly leaned forward and asked, "Is this trip business or pleasure?" I searched, tongue-tied, for an answer. It was a quilting trip, so it must be pleasure. But I was being paid, so was it work? I wasn't sure of the answer, so I explained that I was going back to a museum in New York to give a talk.

"Oh. Ah," he said, nodding sagely. "You must be very important in your field."

An image popped into my mind, and I saw myself in that cartoon in which someone runs across a meadow and leaps over a fence so she can be out standing in that field. As he leaned toward me, I knew what was coming next.

"What is your field?"

Well, quilters know that if you're at a party and someone asks your field, if you say you're a quilter, that person will stand on tiptoe, looking over your shoulder to see if there isn't someone more interesting next to the hors d'oeuvres.

Now sometimes when I answer this question, I say I'm a writer. That sounds a little flaky, and I get a sideways glance. Sometimes I say I'm a teacher. That sounds a little dull, and I can see the eyes glaze over. But this man was strapped in. The red seatbelt light was on, and the flight attendant was standing there watching.

So I said brightly, "I'm a quilter."

"Ah," he said. "Oh." Then, after a pause, he asked, "Why?"

How many times has another quilter asked you this? I'd guess never. Once, at most. We already know the answer. But I tried to explain about connections to quilters from earlier times, connections to quilters all over the country and all over the world. I talked about the power of color and design, the pleasure of making a work from beginning to end. I mentioned creating order out of chaos. He nodded solemnly. Then he leaned forward again for his next query.

"Does anyone need more than one quilt?"

Well, do you know anyone who has only one quilt? It's like having one peanut or one potato chip.

Not possible. And I decided we had plumbed the depths of this conversation. But first I asked him about his work.

"I'm in purchasing at the defense department," he said.

My turn. "Our country has 12,000 nuclear weapons," I said, "And you're asking me if anyone needs more than one quilt?" I got out my earphones and my book and quietly closed the door on further conversation.

The conversation had prompted some questions, however. It did make me consider things I'd taken for granted. "Why do we go to quilt shows and festivals and conferences?" I recently attended one and found the parking lot jammed. The crowds were remarkable, and I was jostled from all sides as I walked past the quilts. The coffee line was long and the food line nearly hopeless. I looked around and wondered, if we were all so eager to quilt, why we were here where it was impossible to do any quilting.

I pondered this for a moment, but it didn't take long to understand our reasons for wanting to be with other quilters. For one thing, nobody asks why we are quilters. No one says, "You paid how much for that fabric?" No one asks, "What are you doing here?" And you don't hear, "You don't really need another (book, pattern, quilt block, class), do you?"

Well, of course you need it. For heaven's sake, you need it for your mental health. It lets you walk just this side of the fine line between sanity and whatever else lurks out there in the dark.

We get together with other quilters for many important reasons. The obvious one is the need to meet with our peers, in the same way that dentists and teachers and entomologists get together. We need feedback from those who value the same things we do.

We attend quilt events for the same reasons we attend classes. Over and over I've watched students come to a workshop and produce incredible work. Of course, they could do it on their own. But they come for something else, something the teacher willingly offers—a confirming presence.

Perhaps the ultimate example of this is the psychiatrist who needs not say a word but who lets the patient do all the talking. He or she provides the confirming presence, or a knowledgeable ear. The student/patient knows that she'll be stopped before making a disastrous move. She goes comfortably forward knowing that someone is there to steer her if she needs direction.

We've all read about the experiments with baby monkeys. If, while growing, they have no contact with adults, no warmth, no voice, no support, they develop slowly, they weaken, and some die. Human babies do much the same when no one talks to them, sings to them, or holds them. Many remain unresponsive and sickly.

We may be called adults, but in a way we're just grown-up babies. Our needs are not that different. We need support and encouragement in our work. And initially that support most often comes from other quilters. Eventually we want critiques, comments, and acceptance. We want to see our work in an exhibit. Our work is an extension of ourselves, an expression of who we are, and it needs to be nurtured and cared for to grow.

And that, I think, is why we go to quilt shows and to exhibits. It's why we attend classes and meetings and guilds. It's why we listen to lectures and read about quilts. All of these activities support us and reinforce our values. And we need them.

So the next time you head off for a quilt event, remember that it is essential to your sanity, to your growth, and to your humanity. You must seek out support for your interests and your passions. Go to the exhibit, get jostled in the crowd, meet a new quilter in the coffee line, and remember that fulfilling your goals makes everything else possible.

QUILTING SAFARI

by Margret Aldrich

There's perhaps no better place to watch people than at a quilt show, where quilters don their favorite quilted vests and chat enthusiastically with friends about their latest projects. In the tongue-and-cheek account that follows, writer Margret Aldrich provides a newcomer's perspective on what she observed when she attended her first big quilt show, the International Quilt Festival in Houston, Texas. Margret lives with her husband in Princeton, New Jersey, where she works in the intellectual property department at Princeton University Press and in the writing center at Princeton University. She has viewed quilts from Australia to Texas, but her favorite spot to see a quilt is at the great Iowa State Fair. She is the editor of two anthologies, This Old Quilt and Once upon a Quilt, both published by Voyageur Press.

The ways of the quilter are very mysterious. Quilters speak of fat quarters and UFOs. They are able to analyze the content of a particular fabric with one deft rub between thumb and forefinger. They match colors effortlessly, prowl quilt-shop aisles tirelessly, and have learned to patch up the worst needle casualty with nary a first-aid kit in sight. Some quilters can even put a dismantled sewing machine back together again—blindfolded. I first became fascinated with these enigmatic creatures while working as an editor of quilting-related books at an independent publisher. As I became more and more familiar with quilters, my fascination with them grew, and I was soon a card-carrying quilt-watcher.

To discover the secrets of any species of quilter, quilt-watchers should strive to observe them in their natural environment. This can be achieved by setting out on a quilting safari. Although no special equipment is necessary for such an expedition, a camera is helpful in documenting the subject's latest patchwork achievement, and binoculars can aid the observer in viewing the minute, marching stitches of a handquilted masterpiece.

For the uninitiated quilt-watcher, sightings of seasoned quilters can be few and far between, as they are known to hole up in workrooms, basements, and even closets, to spend precious hours toiling over intricate projects. A good place to begin the quilting safari is the local discount store or craft shop, where quilters can often be spotted coming out of hibernation to explore the bins of sale fabrics or clearance gadgets. Discount-store shopping is ideal for the quilter who likes to gamble, as nothing is guaranteed to be in stock, but she just might find the perfect lilac calico to match her current piecework design. In the small town where I grew up, the basement of the Ben Franklin's five-and-dime store housed an impressive but little-known stash of quilting supplies. In the cool dimness of the cellar marketplace, tight-lipped quilters cruised the choice fabrics hoping against hope that their secret hunting grounds would be safe for another season.

A more advanced quilt-watcher should, of course, visit a quilt shop. There, rows upon rows of quilters can be found roaming the rows upon rows of fabric, foraging here and there for a particular print or hue. Bolts of cotton stand at attention for inspection, making this the perfect spot for especially organized quilters, or those under a deadline to finish a certain project. In the orderly environment of the well-kept quilt shop, blues are grouped with other blues, reds with reds, and there is a place for all shades of daffodil, rose, and charcoal. Just as every color of fabric lines the aisles, every kind of quilter seems to flock to the local quilt shop, making it a fine nesting place for the avid quilt-watcher.

To truly uncover the inner workings of the quilter's life, however, one should embark on a trek to the center of the quilting universe: the quilt show. Local and statewide quilt shows offer much to study, but the queen of all quilt shows is the International Quilt Festival (IQF) in Houston, Texas. The yearly extravaganza is a mecca for quilters everywhere. Gaggles of festival-goers fly in from China, France, Canada, Japan, Australia, and every country in between. Although they arrive from opposite ends of the world and often speak different languages, all of the attendees seem to understand each other when it comes to the mother tongue of quilting.

At the International Quilt Festival, every skill level and style of quilter can be observed; it is truly a prime location for the ultimate quilting safari. The first type of quilter one will notice is Quiltus holy-cowus, commonly known as the Newcomer. The

Newcomer is branded with the astonished, caught-in-the-headlights gaze of a first-time visitor. The eyes are wide and slightly glazed, a condition that worsens as the four-day event continues, and the mouth is sometimes agape as the magnitude of their surroundings begins to sink in. Hundreds of booths fill the convention center, displaying batiks, hand-dyes, and textured coordinates; books, magazines, and patterns; quilt kits, quilt racks, and vintage swatches. Overwhelmed Newcomers find it difficult to pace themselves, and the opportunistic quilt-watcher may spot them rubbing their tired feet at one of the coveted folding chairs positioned along the convention's outer edges.

Unlike the Newcomer, Quiltus lotsafabricus (aka the Regular) has mastered the sacred quilting mantra "fashion stops at the ankles." Well-seasoned Regulars come to the show wearing the most comfortable, cushiony footwear they can find, and have likely been breaking them in for several months in preparation for Houston. Above the ankles, however, quilting fashion rules, and Regulars are proud as peacocks to model their latest patchwork skirt or quilted jacket. Upon my first visit to the International Quilt Festival, I was dazzled by the plumage of these fabulous creatures, some of whom were wearing attire worthy of an art-gallery wall.

The unique quilting call of the Regular becomes quite recognizable at the IQF. It is a boisterous and sometimes high-pitched squeal or cackle of recognition as one quilter acknowledges another who they may not have seen since the previous year. The joyful "meeting call" of the quilter is often accompanied by a big embrace and a quick peek into one another's shopping bags to see what bounty has accumulated that day.

During the quilt show, Regulars and Newcomers soon become fast friends, as Regulars are very willing to offer expert advice and encouragement. Within my first twenty-four hours in Houston, I met no less than ten different women in the elevator of my hotel who happily shared tips on transportation to the show, what exhibits should not be missed, and what classes looked especially good. Keep your eyes and ears peeled for good deeds and acts of kindness; these are often signs that a Regular is near by.

Other clues that you might be in the presence of a Regular include the following: she has a water bottle close at hand, to stave off the need to pause at the local watering hole for refreshment; peeking from her purse is a schedule of the classes offered that year, with her picks highlighted in Day-Glo yellow; and sometimes, just sometimes, she is accompanied by a personal assistant of the species Ohmy achenback, more commonly called the Husband. While the Husband can be easily mistaken for a shopping cart or a pack mule under the bags and bags of booty piled in his arms, this devoted festival-goer is another important piece of what makes the quilt show tick. Without the Husband, the Regular would not have both hands free to hunt through fat quarters or to greet a fellow quilter on the showroom floor. In return for the Husband's labor at the IQF, his counterpart is likely to pay him back tenfold by accompanying him to a car show or two, or perhaps next year's fishing opener. A more than even trade, to be sure.

Also necessary at any quilting convention are the indispensable chaperones of the show, Quiltus whitegloveous, or Guides. Guides are skillful wranglers of the real stars of our quilting safari—the quilts themselves—pinned up to display-walls like exotic butterflies with wings spread wide open. The Guide's primary identifying mark is a pair of impeccable white gloves, with which she is able to gently handle the quilts. Quilt-watchers should pay close attention to the Guides who mill around the crowded convention hall. If you follow a Guide closely, you may be led directly to the most beautiful quilts in the judging area, as she stops to tag particularly noteworthy quilt specimens with ribbons of purple, blue, and red.

There are countless other kinds of quilters who help make up the diverse patchwork family of the quilt show, including the Casual Quilter, who revisits her drawer of fabric and notions now and then but rarely finishes a project; the Quilting Master, whose wrinkles are only surpassed by the number of hand-stitches she has completed in her lifetime; and the Historian, who can recite each fabric trend and quilting style of the past two centuries. But one of the most precious creatures for quilt-watchers to observe is the Legacy, *Quiltus generationus*, a young quilter who has been taught the craft by her mother or grandmother. The Legacy's hands may not be cal-loused with experience and her stitches may not be perfectly straight, but in her eyes you can see that a bevy of quilting ideas waits to be released. As the Legacy makes her way across the buzzing festival floor, flipping through patterns, examining the appliqué work of a vintage Bird of Paradise quilt and sharing her own experiences and stories with fellow members of her flock, quilt-watchers everywhere can be assured that the wild world of quilting will continue on for generations to come.

LOST

by A. B. Silver

There's a running joke in quilting circles about the husbands who are dragged along to quilt shows and quilt shops. They usually end up toting their wives' purchases or socializing with one another near the entrance of the shop or in the show's food court. When A. B. Silver began writing about his wife Joan's adventures in quilting, he became a voice for the husbands of quilters everywhere. Under the name "Popser" he began posting his musings on the Internet. His columns were eventually published in two books, A Year in the Life . . . 52 Weeks of Quilting and A Year in the Life: 12 Weeks of Sewing. In the following essay, Popser "loses" his wife in a quilt shop, an occurrence that's not at all uncommon.

I lost her in a quilt shop.
Maybe she lost herself. How does one get lost in a small shop? Maybe it wasn't that small. And when did this happen? Last Friday.

Early Friday morning.

I drove her to the shop and stopped the car outside the main door. It was eight-fifty-eight and the shop opened at nine.

"Do you have the cash?" I asked her. She patted the pocket in her pants. She wore heavy-duty pants for heavy-duty shopping. She wore a heavy sweatshirt to protect her in the aisles. Shopping for fabric could be dangerous.

"Yes," she answered.

"And you left the checkbook home?"

"Yes," she said.

"And the credit cards?"

"At home," she said.

"No wallet? Nothing hidden away?"

"I set the limit," she said. "I'm not spending a penny more this time."

"Then go for it," I said. She was ready. No matter how much she might lose control, she had limited herself to how much she could spend. In a fabric store, that was wisdom beyond Solomon's. No changing of her mind. No credit card or checkbook available, even if she saw just one more thing she just had to have.

"I'm off," she said.

"I'll pick you up in an hour. Is that enough time?"

"I need only a couple of things. I'll just be looking around after that."

That was the last I heard from her. I watched her go into the shop and I went a few blocks to Wal-Mart to buy some light bulbs.

When I returned an hour later, five minutes late, I expected her to be out on the sidewalk waiting. She wasn't. I turned off the car's engine and went into the shop to get her.

But she wasn't there. She was nowhere in sight. She wasn't at the display of scissors by the cash register. She wasn't at the display of templates by the front door. "My wife," I said to the cashier when he looked at me. He knew Dear Wife and her quilting money quite well.

He nodded. "She's been shopping here," he said with a grin. I supposed my Darling Shopper had spent her limit and the shop had a good day's income already.

"Still looking around, I guess," I said. He nodded. I went to look for her.

The shop was larger than I thought. Though I had been in many times before, I had never gone beyond the front room where large bolts of fabric filled every bit of floor space. The fabric was arranged by colors along one wall. Specialty fabrics were along another. Reproduction fabrics were on two cases down the center of the shop. Batting sat in rolls in bins near the back.

Everything in the shop was arranged in a way guaranteed to invite the fabric maniac to touch and feel and clutch and buy. I know. I had watched my Darling Wife shop in there too often. But she wasn't in that front room, so I moved through an opening between two bolts of muslin and ducked under a Drunkard's Path quilt that hung down too low from the wall above. Two women stood by a revolving stand of quilting books, but my one-and-only wasn't there either.

"Have you seen my Darling Wife?" I asked. The two women looked me up and down, shook their heads, and busied themselves by opening books up and down the rack.

I went on looking. At one point I thought I found her. "Ohhh, this is nice," I heard, but when I went past a cutting table and turned into an alley between bolts of fabrics covered in stars, all I saw was a young teenager swooning at what was probably her first sight of a hundred fat quarters all in one place.

I moved down another row, around another corner, into a room where the walls were hung with miniature quilts. By now I was getting a bit concerned. I was in some labyrinth even a mythical hero could not get out of, and there was no sign of my happy shopper. I started to push aside bolts of fabric, rolls of fabric, boxes of fabric, thinking she might have fainted at the sight of all these riches and fallen into some dark corner. Or she might have been accidentally rolled up into one of the bolts. Well, it might have happened.

I searched and I searched, but to no avail. The back of the small shop became a dark storeroom of dark corridors, the overwhelming smells of musty and dusty fabrics making me gasp and choke. "Honey, where are you?" I bellowed near and far, but no reply came back. Even the chance of an echo was muted by the miles of fabric.

"May I help you?" came a voice then, out of nowhere. I turned around and looked for the source of the voice. No one.

"I'm over here," the voice said, and I turned to see a mystical shape lift up off the floor, and there, from behind a large box of Olfa mats, a small woman emerged. The shop owner. "I was just checking for water damage. We had a small leak in the ceiling," she explained.

"Have you seen my wife?" I asked, never explaining who she was, what she looked like. I assumed the owner would know her. My good wife spent fortunes at this shop.

"She went out back. I told her to wait until they unloaded, but she was eager to see the new shipment."

"Out back. Eager? New shipment?"

The owner laughed. "She couldn't wait to see what was coming in. She went out to the truck to see the new fabric."

"Where?" I asked, and as she pointed into the depths of this tomb of fabrics, I ran toward a small wedge of daylight in the distance. I brushed past stored cartons of books, bolts of fabric, rolls of batting. I pushed my way past sealed boxes of thread and quilting pins and needles. Then I was out in the alley. And there was the truck. And there she was inside the truck. My Darling Wife was rolling a bolt of solid lavender Hoffman Bali to the side of the truck. I watched, shock stopping me in place. She put the bolt next to another one of William Morris black agapanthus.

(Don't ask!) Then she turned back and saw me.

"Hi, Hon," she said. "Look what I found."

"I've been looking for you," I said as slowly and calmly as I could. Maybe if I wrapped her in a few bolts of duct tape and kept her at home. . . .

"I'm glad you did. You're just in time. I need some extra money to pay for this fabric. Isn't it nice?"

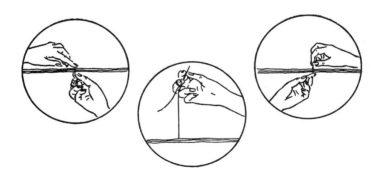

THE AHHHHHHHHHH MOMENT

—by Gail Bakkom

Last May I won a vintage crazy quilt done in feed-sack fabrics for a mere five bucks at an auction. Five bucks! I can still recall the thrill of discovering the quilt under a pile of tattered linens and the joy of acquiring it for such a small sum. Quilt collectors gravitate to antique sales and flea markets, estate sales, and auctions in hopes of having such luck. At each of these sales, where quilts aren't necessarily the main attraction, there's always a chance the collector will find that rare dated quilt in pristine condition to round out a collection or to dress a barren wall in the house. In the following essay, writer Gail Bakkom aptly describes that moment of discovery . . . even if the quilt she buys isn't exactly what she was looking for. Gail, who has been studying and collecting quilts since 1990, is fascinated with the insights they provide into the lives of the makers and with the context of their histories, as well as with their innate beauty and craftsmanship. She also makes her own quilts as a way to relax from her profession as a costume designer and costume shop manager for the Minnesota Opera Company.

As the morning light eased into my room, my eyelids fluttered and lazily closed again. Then they snapped open. Today is the day, I thought, as I stretched to see the alarm clock. Already it was 6:45. I had overslept by an hour. If I jumped into my clothes and walked the dog, I could be back before Jim is up and ready to go. We had been planning this day since the last antique sale and flea market eight months ago. It seemed like ages since we had enjoyed browsing through the hundreds of dealer booths, finding "little" treasures—and sometimes very special ones.

As I hurriedly walked the dog I gave myself the lecture: "You have plenty of quilts. You will not buy a quilt unless it is a dated 1870s one with a pattern that you really like. This is the only date you need to meet your goal of having a dated quilt in each decade from 1840 to 1960. And you don't have space for more quilts!"

Even as I primed myself for this day, I worried that the weather would spoil the fun. Gray clouds swirled above me and the air had that leaden feeling—like it was filled with water and about to explode. It wouldn't be the first time we had experienced a rainout. Of course the dealers inside the building would continue their sale, but I always found the best treasures in the open-air booths.

As we stopped for the traditional coffee and scone on the way, the skies continued to threaten—and I continued my mantra: "Only an 1870s dated quilt, only an 1870s dated quilt." Arriving at the parking lot, we found the threatening weather had affected attendance; we were able to park near the entrance, in case of a downpour. We began to explore the booths, my husband looking for his particular favorite items while I scanned the booths for antique fabric, quilt squares, old needlework magazines and sewing paraphernalia, and, of course, my 1870s dated quilt.

As we slowly worked our way around the outer circle, I saw several quilts. One was very battered (well-loved is the nice way of expressing its condition), and another was a well-done Grandmother's Flower Garden. Since I have several of these, I could appreciate the skill with which the quiltmaker coordinated the patterns with the solids and created a circular motif in a progressive color scheme, beginning with yellow and progressing through the rainbow. The end result was a very pleasing quilt that made great use of those fabulous "happy prints" from the 1930s.

When I caught up with my husband, he quipped, "I thought you would succumb to that one!" I had been so busy studying the quilt that I hadn't even noticed him watching me.

We edged into the second ring and my elation at the thought of the sale began to sag. Not much for me this time, I thought. I hadn't really expected to find the 1870s quilt, but I had hoped for a few of the small items I also collect. Well, at least the rain has held off. There's still hope.

My husband was engrossed in a booth so I wandered ahead until my eye caught a glimpse of velvet fabric hiding under a table. As I bent down to see what it was, the booth owner said, "I keep this pretty well hidden. I don't want just everyone pawing over it, but you seem like you might be really interested." She opened the quilt—it was a stunning crazy one. The black velvet border was beautifully and lavishly embroidered with flowers. A center medallion, a rich burgundy silk, was appliquéd with dimensional flowers. Crazy patches surrounded the center, displaying beadwork, painting, and a multitude of embroidered figures on a variety of dark silk backgrounds.

"It's breathtaking!" I said, barely resisting the need to touch it. "And I'm sure that it is worth a fortune. Unfortunately, I am on a mission to find a dated 1870s quilt and that is all I can consider at this moment."

In a way, it was good that I had made this stipulation for myself because I knew that I would never be able to afford this crazy quilt. I am not a collector with deep pockets, only the taste associated with them. The dealer reluctantly folded up the quilt saying, "If you change your mind, you know where to find me."

Realizing that I had probably spent at least fifteen minutes with her and that gorgeous quilt, I began to search for my husband. We do have a rule that we can't turn a corner and change aisles without finding each other, but the rule doesn't always work and fifteen minutes is a long time to wait to make that turn.

As I searched for my husband, the clouds parted and sunlight streamed through in a beautifully defined ray. Great, I thought, the day will turn out just fine. In front of me the crowd suddenly cleared, and I saw that ray of sunlight falling on a quilt. It just glowed in the light—and sent an arrow into my heart. A long "Ahhhhhhhhhh" escaped my lips as I hurried toward the quilt, my heart pounding, my breathing unsteady. The chrome orange background simmered in the sunlight. Rose of Sharon appliqués bounced merrily across its surface. Solid turkey-red flowers centered the nine blocks. Overdyed green stems flowed in four diagonal directions, topped with red buds that were frosted with a rick-rack-shaped lemon yellow. What an explosion of color! A simply joyous quilt!

I asked the vendor if I could unfold it, and she was happy to help me. The side borders featured the red rose pattern with leaves and vines, while the top and bottom borders contained red buds with that vivid lemon topping, attached to twining vines. When I turned to check out the back, I noticed a little, pink, handwritten note: "My mother made." It almost made me weep.

Looking at it, longing to possess the joie de vivre contained in it, but also remembering my mantra "Only a dated 1870s quilt," my heart fluttered as I did the only thing possible at the moment.

"How much is it?" I asked, hoping against hope that it would be very expensive and I wouldn't be tempted. I was shocked by the answer—not the expense, but the reasonableness of the price. My arms were tired from holding the quilt, but I couldn't bring myself to put it down. That seemed too final. It felt at home in my hands.

Surely the sun breaking through the clouds and shining on this stunning quilt just as I was walking toward it was a sign that I was meant to have it. It was beyond reason—an intervention—and I needed to follow that impulse. Struggling with the words, still at conflict with myself but unable to resist, I said, "I'll take it!" Tension eased out of my body, and feelings of joy and satisfaction flowed through me. To my inner mantra I whispered, "Next time it will be the 1870s quilt, I promise. This was just too special to pass by. I can always find room for just one more quilt."

While paying for the quilt, I remembered my husband. As I turned to look for him, he emerged from the opposite booth, with that knowing look he has. "I've been watching and wondering how long it would take. I knew you wouldn't get by this one."

Chapter Three

HISTORY IN THE MAKING

"A quilt was often the family's diary. Many patterns that are still used today, such as the wagon wheel, star over Texas, log cabin, and cactus flower, originated from wagon train living."

—Eleanor Coerr, *The Josefina Story Quilt*, 1986

THE TRADITION OF QUILTMAKING has a rich history. Early pioneers relied on quilts for warmth, piling several on their beds to keep out the evening chill. Settlers even hung quilts on the walls to minimize drafts and to add color to often drab surroundings. In addition to cleaning house, tending the garden, and making sure there was food on the table, homesteading women made clothes for the family out of feed sacks, yarn, or cloth they wove themselves. Later, when the clothes were well-worn, the women transformed the fabric scraps into quilts, some utilitarian and simple, others both functional and beautiful. For pioneer women, quiltmaking provided a way to keep the family warm, certainly, but it was also one of the only creative outlets and means for self-expression a woman had. And, when living in a barren cabin set in a harsh landscape, a pretty quilt on a wall could make a world of difference. The stories in this chapter harken back to those days, when quilts were carefully stitched by hand.

THE QUILTERS

by Patricia J. Cooper and Norma Bradley Allen

It's difficult to imagine what it must have been
like to live the life of a pioneer, especially on the
unforgiving plains of Texas and New Mexico. In
their award-winning book *The Quilters*, childhood friends Patricia Cooper and Norma Bradley
Allen capture the hardships of the settlers
through the eyes of the quilters they interviewed
for the book in the early 1970s. The quilts these
women made added color, joy, and warmth to
their lives, and most importantly, they gave them
something interesting to do to fill the lonely
hours. Molly Newman and Barbara Damashek
later adapted the book into a musical, which was
nominated for several Tony Awards.

Patricia Cooper taught at the University of
California at Berkley until her death in 1987.
Norma Bradley Allen lives on an old farm in
Cedar Hill, Texas, where she continues to write.

L ate in the summer of 1974 we were on the high
plains of Texas, looking for a little farm where
Mrs. Wilman quilted and kept chickens. We

had been told she had quilts from three generations out there and that she still quilted daily herself. The house was a small, wooden, three-room, white painted structure set right down in the dirt with a few shrubs around. As far as you could see in any direction was flat plowed land. The house had been there a long time by local standards, probably built right on the site of the dugout of the original homestead. Mrs. Wilman peered through the screened door at us. We explained that Mrs. Hammond had sent us, and that we were looking at quilts and talking with people about them. The strained suspicion disappeared from her face and she unlatched the door to the screened porch which stretched the length of the house front.

We stayed three days. She could make the rooms come alive with her talk. As she related her life and the history of her family, all the themes, fragments, fleeting insights merged into a whole for us. We saw the pioneer woman and the artist.

"I'm making grape jam. You'll have to talk while I work. I was the oldest child of a family that had settled in West Texas in 1890. My folks came from Springfield, Missouri. They wanted more land, their own land. My daddy used to say, 'I don't know anything more satisfying than your own land as far as the eye can see.' They were after acres of their own. In the Southwest then, if you were willing to work hard, you could make a fortune. My mama was newly married and came from a big, white house in Springfield with elm trees in the front yard and lilacs all around. She was for moving west to where they could get ahead and get something for the kids. She was lively and had been a tomboy in her family. I don't think she was afraid of anything, but she always said nobody could imagine then what you was getting into out on the plains of Texas. She hadn't even talked to anyone about what it was like in this area before they set out. She told about starting out in the covered wagon with one bedstead and a lamp given to them by her mother, and all the quilts she had made for her hope chest. They had two wooden trunks full of tools, seed, and utensils for the house; Dad had his plow knocked down inside the wagon and his hoes, shovels, and ax strapped to the side. On the back they tied a cow, and a team of mules pulled the wagon.

"Mama had her piece bag with her on the whole trip and was working on this Star of Bethlehem I have here. Later I come to call it the Lone Star when I

76

made it. She was still working like she used to at home with little tiny fine pieces out of that quilt bag. By the time she got to the edges of the star she was piecing pieces to get it finished. From then on, until neighbors moved nearby in 1910, she was piecing from our worn-out clothes and work clothes with a little bit of fabric thrown in from when Dad got to town and could afford some yardage.

"She used to talk a lot about that first year. Seems it stood out in her memory so clear, and that was the year I was born.

"She used to tell how when they come finally to the homestead and the wagon stopped she felt so lonely. There was emptiness as far as the eye could see. How could a human endure? There wasn't even anything to hide behind. The color was dull yellow and brown. The sky was always changing. Out here you notice the colors always changing because there is nothing else to look at but the things you make right around you and the sky. You can see the weather coming . . . dust storms, northers, rain, tornadoes, and twisters. In those days you could see anything that stood up against the horizon. The fence rows and windmills stood out for miles, and in that time you knew where folks had settled by the windmills. The houses was built underground and called dugouts. Or they would build a half dugout, finishing the top part with lumber and sod and tar paper.

"My papa worked on the well and building the windmill first. They had to have water. He had help from the Thompsons, who rode two days to get to our place. Mama said one of the great pleasures of her life was putting her face in that first bucket of water.

"The first summer Mama worked with shovel and pick to build the dugout. Papa was out there to start a ranch, and he went right off looking for cattle to make a small herd. He began to put in feed crops right after they put down stakes. He would dig when he could but Mama worked at it every day. That and the garden. She was putting in seed too. She says most evenings she barely had strength to get her clothes off before she fell asleep. They could hardly bear to eat or fix food they were so tired.

"Mama used to say, 'Don't stop now or you'll never get going.' When we had a long, hard job coming up she would say, 'Mary, we won't sit down today.' Sometimes when the work would get too hard, I would ask 'Why?' And she would say real quiet,

'Because you just have to. There's nothing for it but to do it.'

"When the dugout was just big enough to stand up in and braced with wood, she put in the bedstead and the quilts and had a good day's rest. Papa made a shelf for the lamp. There it sits over there on my table now.

"Mama said she thanked the Lord that the first dust storm didn't come up till late that summer. She would have turned right around and gone home if she'd seen one first off. It was just like now, you know, only worse because the farms, sodbusters, hadn't planted much yet, and the sand was mixed with plowed dirt. Oh Lord. At the horizon the dust came up like a yellow band between earth and sky and then it kept on rising and rolling toward you till you were right inside it. Small and large twisters and tumbleweeds all mixed up with it and the sand sifted into every pore in your body. I always know one is coming because the light changes. It gets yellow and real still all around. When the sand hits, it's dark and cold. She hated being underground but she said at least you didn't hear the wind so loud. The sand would sift in through the door until you felt buried alive. No wonder they got out of those dugouts so fast. Folks never lived in one any longer than it took to get some time, lumber, and tar paper together.

"The first time Mama was left alone was when Papa hitched up the wagon to go after firewood. Up in the breaks there was wood and you could haul back enough for the winter in one trip. It was a week in all, there and back. That was late September. Mama had her garden in and she was plowing more land for corn when the first dust storm came up. The wind blew for three days so hard and the air was so full of dust that she had to tie a rope around her waist to get out to feed and milk the cow. There was nothing else but to endure it. She had never heard sounds like was in the wind. She took to quilting all day every day. She used to say, 'If I hadn't had the piecing, I don't know what I would have done.' There was nobody to talk to and nowhere to go to get away from the wind except underground. She got to worrying about freezing to death in the winter. She used to laugh when she told it, how you never saw anyone quilt so fast in your life.

"Mama's best quilts were her dugout quilts because that was when she really needed something pretty. She made a Butterfly and a Dresden Plate and a Flower Basket during those two years in the dugout. After a while she got to like the sound of the wind, if it didn't go on too long, and she could get real soothed with that sound and the needlework at night sitting by the lamp. She made the Basket for Papa. She started the Butterfly in that first dust storm all alone. She couldn't see how the garden was gonna survive the wind and she knew the trees she had planted were done for. One lived though; that pecan right out there. I water it every day. The Butterfly was free and fragile. It was the prettiest thing she could think of. She knew I was coming along and the Butterfly was for me.

"She didn't want a baby to be born in the dugout, but I was. And it was one more winter before they got aboveground. She said she just wasn't gonna live underground with a baby, but they couldn't get crop or cattle money and the lumber was expensive. That second winter was hard. They planned the house and she quilted everything she could get her hands on, just for warmth. This house was made just like she planned it."

We looked around us and realized she had laid the groundwork for the house with her quilts. If she had not quilted and planned quilts through those bad times, maybe she would have been planning how to get out of that country. The quilts were her base and from them she planned and completed her next project, the house. At each step she sank her roots deeper into the earth.

At each level she changed, built her surroundings. She structured her surroundings. Oh yes, then the community came next. Roots reaching out from one ranch to the next, from one house to the next . . . a whole network, a grid of support. A quilt. In our imagination we rose over the house and looked down on the patches of land spread flat out like a good quilt as far as the eye could see.

  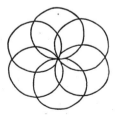

EXCERPT FROM
DOUBLE WEDDING RING

by Patricia Wendorf

When I stumbled upon an excerpt from
Patricia Wendorf's *Double Wedding Ring* in
Quilt Stories, a wonderful collection of writings
published by the University of Kentucky Press
in 1994, I found the tale so compelling that I
couldn't bring myself to put the book down. In
Double Wedding Ring, British author Patricia
Wendorf tells the story of Rhoda Greypaull
Salter, a widow and settler from England who
struggles to raise her three children and run
the family's Wisconsin farm on her own. In
this excerpt, told through a series of diary
entries, Rhoda explains how she came to know
Captain James Kerr Black, the man who would
become her second husband. Patricia Wendorf
based *Double Wedding Ring* on the history of
her own family, which came to the United
States from England in the 1800s. The irregular
spellings inherent in the original manuscript
have been retained here for authenticity.

DECEMBER 20

Johnnie Vickery brings his mother over to us in the cutter. Never was the sound of sleigh bells sweeter or more welcome. Elizabeth and I have much catching up to do. It is three whole weeks since last we were together. She remarks that I look weary, what is small wonder! She offers to send Willum to me to help out.

"It is such a kind thought," say I, "but my Georgie is so set on proving himself. He would be mortally hurt if Willum came here. He is touchy at present over any outside aid."

Elizabeth looks troubled. She begins to talk of the three Englishmen who lately came to Suamico. Their house and barn, she says, was finished just before the deep snows fell, what is fortunate for them. "Altho," says my sister, "there can be very little homeliness and comfort in a place where three men 'bach' together." "Mr. Goodman," she adds, "is a poor-looking specimen and never likely to get wed. Mr. Sutton, on the other hand, is qwite presentable while Mr. Hopkins is downright handsome, having all his own teeth, and a full head of hair even tho' he is middle-aged."

"Perhaps," I say, "they do not wish to get wed. In fact, it is my belief that if a man is still unmarried at the age of forty then he is a lost cause and best left by himself. Such men become set in their bachelor ways, they grow selfish and self-opiniated."

Elizabeth gives me a keen look and begins to speak of other matters.

For some time past it would seem that Suamico folk have wished to build a church where the Episcopalians might worship in comfort. The women of the congregation have formed a society to raise money. Jim Black is their Treasurer. He himself, says Elizabeth, has already made a contribushun of five hundred dollars.

"He does not," say I, "give the impreshun of being so well-off."

"Oh," says Elizabeth, "Jim is not the man for outside show. But remember, Rhoda, he is a foreman-logger. Such men command high wages in the lumber camps. When the season ends, Jim never goes on a drinking spree with the other 'jacks' into Green Bay. He comes home straightaway to his farm, and saves his money." She nods. "Yes, yes! Jim Black is prudent. He is probably among the best-off of all the farmers hereabouts."

"It is easy," I say, "for a non-drinking bachelor to hoard his gold. How else should he spend it? He certainly wastes little on clothing and home comforts!"

Elizabeth smiles. "Perhaps he has never had the chance yet? Perhaps he is longing to spoil some lucky woman?" I make no answer.

My sister asks how long it is since I have done any qwilting. Not for some time, I tell her. She says what a pity, since I am qwick and skilful at the task.

"We had hoped," she says, "to hold a Qwilting Bee. A fine patchwork qwilt will fetch as much as fifty dollars. It would help a good deal towards the funds for our new church. But in weather such as this it will be months before a group of us can meet together. I hesitate to ask when you are so hard-pressed in the yard and dairy . . . ?"

"But I would love to make a qwilt!" say I. "It is a soothing occupashun on a winter's evening." I point out our tablecloth and cushions.

"These are all the work of Rosa. As you know, I learned plain qwilting in England. But Rosa is very skilled in the American fashun of patchwork."

My sister says: "I have a customer in mind, Rhoda. One who will pay a good price for a fine qwilt."

I laugh. "Do not tell me who it is. The Suamico ladies are such skilled needlewomen. To know her name would make me nervous."

Rosa comes into the room and we tell her of the project. She runs to find our scraps bag. We spend a happy hour sorting thru' the pieces.

December 23

Elizabeth comes with news that the doctor is calling once again at the Black Farm. Jim Black, she says, now has his hands full, what with caring for his sick brother, and all the chores of house and yard. "It would," she says, "be a Christian act on your part, Rhoda, to go across and see them."

When evening comes, I fill a satchel with jars of my preserves, and some cakes fresh-baked by Rosa. I bid Georgie to take them to Matthew Black. On his return, my son's report causes me to worry. Matt has developed a deep and wracking cough and is most unwell. Furthermore, snow begins to fall as Georgie makes his way home. I am wakeful in the small hours. From my window I see that a lamp burns night-long over at the Black Farm. The wind gets up and I am fearful of a blizzard.

DECEMBER 24

It is my birthday! I am forty-four years old, but no time to ponder on it! Once again we awaken to drifted snow and blocked trails. We are obliged to dig our way out towards the cow barn. We go about our tasks with heavy hearts. There is no doubt that we are once more qwite cut-off from all our dear ones. The storm rages round the house and barn, the path being blocked almost as fast as we can clear it. By evening we are all worn-out, even Jon, who is beside himself with worry for his feathered flock, and so must come with us where 'ere we go! As I pen these words my little boy falls fast to sleep across the bearskin rug before the fireplace. Georgie carries him to bed.

CHRISTMAS DAY 1874

The storm is over. We awaken to clear skies and starshine, tho' the frost still deep. We gather in the kitchen where Georgie has already fired the stove and has coffee boiling. He has a glum look. "First time," he says, "that I was ever sent out to work on a Christmas Day!"

"Well I'm sorry, Georgie," I tell him, "but unfortunately our Holsteins take no heed of the season."

Rosa is also low in spirit.

"I was so looking forward to dinner at Aunt Elizabeth's. It's so much nicer being with them. They're still a proper family." She sends me an apologetic look. "Well, you know what I mean, Mama. They still have a father."

Oh yes, I do indeed know what she means. At this time of year, more than any other, I remember George and our first years together, when Eddie was a small boy, and all our lives seemed to stretch out before us. I recall my dear husband's premonition that his would be a short span; and poor Ed, cut down in the flower of his young manhood. Tears come to my eyes. The children see this and are contrite. Georgie begins to help Jon put on his many layers of warm clothes. Rosa clears away the breakfast dishes. She says in a bright voice: "I know what we can do! We'll begin to make that qwilt, Mama! We'll start this very evening!"

We say a short prayer together before setting out upon our chores.

The path between house and barn has stayed clear overnight. But the half-mile of trail between us and Elizabeth, and to James Black's, is still blocked by drifts.

The thought of the qwilt qwite lifts our spirits. We talk it over thru' the milking. I say: "Better I think if we stick to the sort of sewing I know best."

"Oh no," she cries, "this customer will want bright colours and a bold pattern. After all, Mama, if a person is willing to pay fifty dollars into the church fund, then we must come up with something more romantic than your plain qwilting."

"I had never," say I, "thought of qwilts and romance both together."

"In American families," my girl tells me, "a qwilt is so much more than a warm covering in winter. It is a symbol. There are engagement qwilts and bridal qwilts, and each has its own speshul pattern."

"You seem to know a lot about it."

"Oh, indeed I do, Mama! You recall when we first came to this house and I made throws and cushions? It was Aunt Elizabeth's friends who showed me how to piece the patterns, and each one has its own name. There's Grandmother's Flower Garden and Courthouse Steps, Barn Raising and Log Cabin, Drunkards Path and Cathedral Window, and, oh, a whole heap more! Some of the designs," says Rosa, "have hidden meanings."

We finish the milking and go to the dairy. Georgie comes into the barn. He is ready to clean up and put down fresh straw. He hears our talk. He says: "There's an old qwilting-frame up in the attic. I'll get it down for you when we're all through with chores."

We almost forget that it is Christmas Day, and that we are isolated by the snow. The work goes with a will! After supper is done with, Georgie brings to us the frame. Rosa cleans it with a damp cloth. It is in perfect order. Already, Jon has sorted out our scraps bag. He makes heaps of each separate colour, but Rosa says we are far short of what is needed. We go each one to our highboy drawers and cupboards, and find odd garments, rarely worn. I have a few bolts of plain calico, bought in Green Bay when we first came here. All together, says my girl, it should be suffishent!

We sit around the kitchen table, the frame beside us. Now comes the great decishun. What pattern should we follow?

"I am in your hands," I say to Rosa. "It is you who knows all about this American fashun of patchwork."

"Well," says she, "there is a most romantic qwilt, always in demand. It's not the easiest to make, but oh, it looks so fine when finished!"

Georgie sends his sister a very hard look, and I think he is about to speak, but then he would seem to bite back on the words. Rosa's cheeks are flushed, her eyes a-sparkle, her dark curls shining in the lamplight. I see how pretty she has grown.

"Since we don't know," she goes on, "who our customer will be, it may be safer to choose a tradishunal qwilt. The one I have in mind is called Double Wedding Ring. It's a repitishun of linked circles made of patterned fabrics against a plain background. Oh, Mama, it looks so elegant, do say that we can do it!"

I am doubtful, but do not wish to spoil her pleashur. I say: "If you are sure about this?"

She turns to face her brother. "You'll help us, won't you, George? The Vickery boys help Aunt Elizabeth with her qwilts on winter evenings, and it's all in a good cause."

DECEMBER 27

More snow falls. We turn to our new evening occupashun, thankful for the interest. I pay Jon two bits for one night's needle-threading. He is kept busy with three of us to thread for. Georgie, after some small struggle, takes up a needle. He is slow but neat. We decide, in the end, on a background of lilac-coloured calico, with the rings of the pattern worked in pieces of flowered and checkered cotton. To my surprise I find this American patchwork a most calming occupashun.

JANUARY 1

Robert and Elizabeth get through to us this forenoon! They are concerned that we spent Christmas by ourselves but I tell them we were not too low in spirit. Rosa shows them our qwilt and they are full of praise. We spend two happy hours together. They say that, as they came, a party of neighbours were clearing the trail up to the Black Farm.

JANUARY 4

No more snow. The cleared trails stay open. My conshunce troubles me on behalf of Matthew, tho' truth to tell we could not have reached him until now.

Our morning chores once done, I say to Rosa: "We must go over to the Black Farm." I pack a basket. We take soup and cakes, and a batch of my fresh muffins, with a crock of our new butter to be melted on them. George bides to home with Jon.

The door of the loghouse is opened to us by Captain Black. I am shocked at his appearance. He has grown so gaunt in these past weeks. More still am I alarmed at Matthew. I go into the rear room to find that he has taken to his bed again and looks mortal sick. I say to Jim Black: "Whatever happened? I thought your brother to be almost recovered when I last came here. He was sitting out and on the mend."

Captain Black is very low, has quite lost his old style of command, and is so humbled in his spirit that I am driven to comfort him.

"I am sure it was not your fault that he had a set-back. Your care of him is so devoted. But he does not seem at all well."

"It was the blizzard, Mrs. Salter. Matt said that he was better. He would come out to help me with the yard work tho' I said he shouldn't."

Even as we speak, a bout of coughing wracks poor Matthew. We rush to help him.

I say to Captain Black: "This is bronchitis! We need to get moisture into the air to ease his breathing! You must keep a kettle boiling on the stove at all times."

I look around me. The little house is in a sad state, the sink piled-up with unwashed dishes, the floors unswept, and Matthew's bed all rumpled-up and needing clean sheets.

"Bring me fresh linen," I say, "and lift your brother for a moment while I put it beneath him." I remake the poor man's bed, for which he thanks me. As I do, I notice the poorness of his blankets, which are heavy but give little warmth. "It is a qwilt you really need," I tell him.

"Our mother made qwilts when we were children back in Kingston," says Matthew. "Oh my, but they were nice and cosy."

Jim Black grins at his brother. "And you shall have a qwilt again right soon! Elizabeth tells me that Mrs. Salter here has gotten started on my order."

He turns to me. "I shall pay my fifty dollars to the church fund just as soon as you have put the last stitch in, ma'am!"

By this time I am toasting muffins at the fire. A burning colour floods my face, what I pray he will put down to my occupashun.

I am too mortified to answer. I recall the qwilt design of the Double Wedding Ring. Such patterns, my daughter says, are meant to carry hidden meanings. It is an American tradishun. Well the message of my qwilt cannot possibly be clearer, can it? For a widow to stitch such a pattern for a bachelor's bed surely is unheard of?

I say in a faint voice: "My sister said she had a customer waiting. I did not guess that it was you sir." My anger drives me to be busy. I set about me with broom and duster. I wash up dishes while Rosa feeds Matt with a tray of soup and buttered muffins.

I say to Jim Black: "Better that you go outside and chop-up wood, sir! You are such a large man. You all but fill this little cabin."

JANUARY 6

Our work on the qwilt now has an urjent feel about it. What is silly, since yesterday I took three of my own plain old qwilts across to the Black Farm for Matthew's use.

It is Jim Black who harps on about the new one I am making. He has, so he says, a superstitious feel about it. That it alone will see the turning-point for Matthew.

"What nonsense!" say I. "It is good medicine your poor brother needs!" I pick up the doctor's bottle of red-coloured liquid, and sniff at it.

"This is of little use to a man in Matt's condishun. It will only serve to irritate his damaged stomach. Now I have a remedy, Captain Black, what will sooth his cough, and put new life back in him." (Truth to tell, I needs must turn the conversashun since talk of qwilts now sends the colour burning to my face.)

"What we really need," I go on, "is a number of lemons. Since we have none then a quart of Elizabeth's apple-cider will do just as well. To the cider you add glycerine and honey in the qwantities that I will show you. This mixture to be used as needed, one or two teaspoons at a time. The honey has life-giving qwalities and will not harm Matt's stomach."

I see by his baffled look that the cabin holds neither glycerine nor honey.

"Oh, never mind," I cry. "I will make the linctus for you, and send Georgie over with it!"

JANUARY 10

Jim comes across each morning to help me with the milking and churning, while Rosa goes over to minister to Matthew and give him breakfast. There is no doubt that a man's strong arm makes all the difference on a farmstead. Find myself less tired by evening, and so able to work longer on our qwilt.

Jim turns out to be a first-rate dairyman. I was not sure at first if we could work together, but so far all is harmonious between us. He points out that I am running short of winter fodder, but forbears to menshun that this lack is due to my own wilful wish to grow clover rather than com. He loads up his cutter with sacks of flour and grain, grown in his own fields, suffishent to see me thru' until harvest comes around again.

JANUARY 15

Today my George is seventeen years old. We make the house festive with paper-chains and green boughs. After all, we have missed Christmas! Between the morning and evening milking I take an hour or two to look at my appearance. My gown of crimson silk with the narrow bodice and deep-frilled skirt, still lies in tissue-paper. Rosa irons it while I wash my hair. She is critical lately.

She says: "Why must you always dress your hair so severely, Mama? It would wave so nicely if only you would not scrape it back behind your ears." She seized the comb and begins to braid, but loosely. She coils the braid and pins it high upon my head. I look in the mirror. It is not a fashun I am used to, but the result is not displeasing. The hair indeed waves softly round my face giving me a *younger* look. Even Jon has has noticed. When I am dressed in the crimson silk he says: "You look real pretty, Mama!"

The road is open between the three farmsteads. The whole Vickery family comes over, even little Robert who soon falls to sleep, and is laid in Rosa's bed. Poor Matthew, tho' still too weak to leave his bed, *incists* that Jim shall join us. We are a merry party! We drink my boy's health in apple-cider. Our table groans beneath the food set out upon it. I look around the dear faces of my relatives and friends, and know that life is good.

"Another toast!" I cry. "Let us drink to this great land of America, and especially to the State of Wisconsin where we have all found such a welcome, and a good home."

My eyes are drawn often towards Jim, who is looking uncommon fine. He wears trousers of a tight cut in dark-green plaid, with a short jacket of black velvet trimmed with silver buttons. His shirt is of silk with a frilled and lace-edged jabot. His shoes black-patent with silver buckles. I whisper to Elizabeth: "What is that outfit?"

She says: "It is the *tradishunal* Scottish. He wears it only on very *speshul occashuns*."

We sit long at table. The men ask if they may smoke. Cigars are lit and there is the rich smell of good tobacco. The talk winds around to the time when we older folk were also seventeen.

Georgie says: "And what were you doing, Captain, when you were my age?"

"Why," says Jim, "that's just the age when I left the home farm and started lumbering. My father died when Matt and I were children. Years later, when Mother passed away there was nothing to hold us— we just lit out with our few belongings—Matt and me." He grinned. "That's when we came to America and met up with you folks."

Robert says: "That must have been a hard life."

"I was a young man in a young country. At the age of eighteen I was riding the log-rafts down the Ottowa River."

Georgie leans forward in his chair, his interest caught: "I've heard about life in the logging-camps. Is it really as tough as it's made out?"

"It's a mite more civilised in these days, but I guess it's not all that different. Being snow-locked is the worse thing, when mail and extra supplies can't get through. That's when a foreman needs to be real strict."

"How," I ask, "does a man come to be a logger?"

"Well it's not always voluntary. It's like this—the company agents mostly set up shop in a saloon. When recruiting starts there's a brisk flow of free whisky. There's many a youngster who comes in looking for his buddy, or just to warm himself before the fire—and he wakes up hours later in a sleigh on the backroads to the pineries—and with a thundering headache!"

Rosa says: "Did that happen to you?"

"No. I went of my own free will. I'd watched the men who ride the log-jams in the spring. It looked to me like a fine adventure. But such men are part of a skilled crew. I had first of all to learn to be a logger, before I could be a white-water man." Jim grinned at Georgie. "The camp life is pretty dull. You get up in darkness, and you come back in darkness. There's no home comforts. Fifty, maybe sixty, men to every bunkhouse, a couple of box stoves with wet socks and other garments hung on lines above 'em. There's always a card game going on, but never for money. Gambling stirs up hard feelings in the men, likewise alcohol makes 'em slow and stupid. There's always one who can play the flute or the harmonica, so we sometimes have a sing-song. Sundays is for letterwriting and mending ripped clothes. Nobody shaves. Most men sleep all Sunday through, only waking up when the cookhouse gong sounds."

I say: "What kind of food is served in such condishuns?"

He smiles at me. "Why nothing so excellent, ma'am, as the meal you've given us this evening. But the camp food is good and a decent cook is worth gold. There's always salt pork and beef, potatoes and baked beans. Pies and cake are favourite—washed down with strong tea. Sometimes the cook will barter sugar with the Indians for a few pails of blueberries or cranberries."

Georgie says: "Tell us more about the log-drive."

"That's the most dangerous time of all," says Jim. "First of all you have to get your logs down to the river. I send a couple of men out overnight to sprinkle water on the track, so that the sleighs will pull well on the icy surface. We calk the horses' shoes—ah but that's a fearsome sight, to see the great horse-drawn sleighs loaded up with timber! Then we wait for warmer weather. When the snow melts the river level rises. The stacked-up logs are rolled down to the water, and that's a risky job too. A log-jam is the worst of all. There's many a young man lost his life working to free a jam."

"How long," I ask, "does it take to get the logs down to the mills?"

"Why, several weeks, ma'am. The cookshack goes with us. We sleep in tents along the riverbank as we move downstream. Those nights are awful cold, and a man gets pretty well soaked through working on the river. I've known mornings in the early spring when my clothes were frozen solid to my body. There's no time to stop and dry things. Just got to keep moving every day."

I say: "It's a wonder that you're still here to tell your story!"

"It's a job for strong men," says he, "who are not afraid of hard work."

"What happens," asks George, "when the drive is over?"

Jim draws on his cigar. His dark eyes twinkle. "You've been hearing talk, I don't doubt, about the binges that occur when the lumbermen hit Green Bay and Escanaba, with six months' pay burning in their pockets? Well, I'll tell you. The most of them stories are true! Oh I won't mislead you folks. Matt and I went on a binge or two when we were young blades. But I've been Mr. Tremble's foreman for a good few years now, and I've learned some sense along the way. Put it down to my Presbyterian upbringing, or that I come from Scottish stock—but I'm real careful with my dollars these days!"

He looks at me across the table. He says: "Guess I'm as respectable and qwiet a man as any gently brought-up lady could ever want?"

The colour rises in my face so that my cheeks match the crimson of my gown. They are all watching me. I say, to change the subject, and because it is the first thing that comes into my head: "Perhaps you would like to see the qwilt, sir? It is more than half-way finished."

He says in a most *seerious* tone: "Show it to me, Rhoda, when you have it all done."

FEBRUARY 10

No entry made since George's birthday. We work every evening on the qwilt. I go to visit Matthew most days. He improves, but slowly. George now talks admiringly of Jim, as does Rosa. Indeed, I also see him in a different light since learning more about him. To know is to understand. Allowance can be made for the roughness of a man's appearance when the cause is hard work and condishuns. How I regret my high words about his beard when he came back from last spring's log-drive! It was, after all, a very fine beard, black and curling. Jim is altogether a most imposing figure of a man, and qwite the strongest I have ever known.

Watching him when he helps out around my yard and cow barn I am *amazed* at the ease with which he lifts bales and sacks. The work goes twice as fast with Jim's help. The little I can do for Matthew seems small return for so much kindness. I must go now to take my place at the qwilting-frame. Rosa is already sewing. Georgie grows speedy with the qwilting needle, and Jon kept busy threading for us all.

My Double Wedding Ring qwilt is almost finished.

FEBRUARY 17

Elizabeth comes over in the cutter, bringing little Robert with her. Jon and he play well together. My sister, being skilled at the American patchwork, helps to put the final touches to our qwilt. We spread it out across the kitchen table. The linked rings are in shades of blue with here and there a touch of red and yellow, flowered and striped patches, matched carefully by Rosa, who is the artist among us. The rings show up fine and bold against the lilac-coloured background. Elizabeth looks at me with meaning. She says:

"Oh my, but Jim will surely love this qwilt!"

I say: "It is meant to bring good health to Matthew. Jim has this fanciful noshun about it. That it will be for a turning-point."

Elizabeth smiles in that secretive way of hers that tells me she has prior knowledge. "Oh I don't doubt but it'll be a turning-point for somebody!" says she.

I begin to talk fast about my butter. "When the weather eases," I tell her, "I intend to sell my whole stock in the Green Bay butter market where the price is better."

My sister lays her hand upon my forearm; she pats the finished qwilt. "You were ever good at hiding your true feelings, Rhoda; but do be wary of hiding them too well! The men of this country are simple and direct. Without encouragement of some kind a suitor might well become fainthearted and give up the chase. Espeshully if he should be a bachelor of mature years, and not used to women's ways."

I gather up the tea-cups. I say: "How nice it is for Jon to have your little boy to play with. I fear he is too much with us older folk."

Elizabeth shakes her head, gathers up her child, and drives away.

February 19

It is in these candle-hours that I am lonesome. The wind roars tonight about the house, the children are long a-bed, and here sit I, my accounting ledgers spread out upon the kitchen table. But I have no heart for adding figures. I am lower in spirit than I have been since we left Chicago.

Jim comes over to help George put new roofing shingles on the hog-house. When he is all done he comes into the kitchen. I show him the completed qwilt.

I say: "Well, here it is—and I hope it is what you wanted."

I can see he is impressed. He stands back a pace. "Magnificent," he cries.

I wait, but it seems that the one word is all that is to pass his lips. I say, in a desperate fashun: "It is the Double Wedding Ring design. It is not easy to do." I try to make the words sound offhand, as if the whole matter means nothing to me. After all I still have some pride left.

"It is a Bridal Qwilt," I say. I think he must surely take heart from all of this, but he stands tall and broad and mute.

The silence between us is *awful*. I cannot bear it. I begin to bundle the qwilt fast together. I push it into his hands.

I say, rather coldly, "Well, I hope it looks well on Matthew's bed." Jim turns and walks away.

As he goes I cry out: "Now, don't forget, will you? You owe the sum of fifty dollars to our church building fund!"

FEBRUARY 22

Meetings between myself and Captain Black grow more awkward by the day. He loses all his former boldness and is now as tongue-tied as my George gets when Rosa's friends come calling. It is very vexashus since I am now more than a little fond of him.

FEBRUARY 23

I know that he wants me. It is in his voice, his look, whether or not he will admit it. He just cannot seem to broach the subject. Oh, whatever shall I do? It is up to me to bring him to the point. But how best to do it without loss of face, or seeming forward?

February 28

Trails are now open between all farmsteads, altho' snow still lying deep in fields and on the backroads. The raising of funds for our new Episcopal church is becoming urjent. Young couples who have planned to wed at Eastertide must go all the way to Green Bay if they would marry in their family faith. A "Basket Soshul" is to be held by the ladies of our congregashun. This is a very pleasant and romantic American means of raising funds for a good cause. The habit is for the ladies and girls to each one decorate a box or basket and fill it with refreshments for two. On a certain evening the community assembles in the school room, and each box or basket is auctshuned-off with the men and boys bidding on them. Of course, no one is allowed to know the owner of these lovely boxes, since they are all carried in great secrecy in a Brown Paper Bag.

I say at first that I will not have time for all of this. Truth to tell I am downhearted and lack inclinashun.

But Rosa will not let the matter rest. "You cannot," she cries, "be the only woman in the congregashun who has no luncheon box to auctshun!"

I think long and deep about the matter. There is a qwantity of lilac calico left over from the qwilt, and several pretty patches. I begin to sew. I make the Double Wedding Ring pattern. When a suffishent length is put together I cover my basket with it. When the evening of the auctshun comes, I fill the basket to the brim with the cakes and cookies that he fancies most. I go with my children to the school room, and place my brown paper bag among fifty or so others. When the people are assembled the paper bags are taken off, and the baskets and boxes lined up upon a trestle-table. Mine looks most distinctive.

If James Black does not recognise my message this time, then he is not worthy of my feelings for him!

Oh brave words, Rhoda!

When the moment comes and the bidding begins I am as ankshus and fluttery as any schoolgirl. Suppose he should bid for someone else's basket? I think I could not bear it.

When my effort is put-up a silence falls. The bidding starts. It comes from the far side of the room.

I recognise the voices of Matthew and Jim. They call for some long time, one against the other. Cheering breaks out among the company as the competishun grows fierce. When the figure called by Jim reaches twenty-five dollars, Matthew cries: "Enough! I can't match that!"

Everybody starts to laughing. There is much good-natured teasing. It is clear to all that the contest was arranged between them.

The custom is that the winner of a basket should sit together with the maker of it, and eat the lunch provided. As the young men claim the makers of their prizes, I see how many a romance is begun in this way. The winner of my particular prize comes striding towards me. His face is flushed and he is smiling broadly. We retire to a secluded corner and sit down together.

He says: "I shall treshur this basket all my life, Rhoda! I recognised your pattern straight away."

He looks deep into my eyes, he takes my hand.

He says: "Will you not share a double wedding ring of gold with me?"

WOMEN WHO QUILT

by Linda Northway Kosfeld

Over the past twenty years, the Minnesota Quilt Project has been documenting the state's quilts, dating from settlement until 1975. The story of those quilts and of the quiltmakers and family members who treasure them is related on the pages of *Minnesota Quilts: Creating Connections with Our Past* published by Voyageur Press in 2005. In this essay, writer Linda Northway Kosfeld steps back in time as she travels the state gathering the quilts to be photographed for the book. She relates a few stories about the quilt owners she met and the stories they told her about their beautiful quilts.

Linda has been a quilter for more than twenty-five years. She lives in Bloomington, Minnesota, where she shares her home with three resident cats and with various foster cats and kittens waiting for adoption. Linda has two daughters: Alissa, who lives in Chicago with husband Dean and children Louie, Will, and Mary; and Katie, who lives in Kansas City.

I love studying road maps and planning an itinerary, preferably on back roads through small towns. My ancestors lived and worked on farms and in small towns, so trips along rural roads to visit grandparents and aunts and uncles were part of my childhood. Now when I drive through the country I savor the views of fields green with crops in summer or dotted with dry stubble after harvest. I watch for weathered old barns no longer in use, listing to one side, and I wonder how much longer they will stand before a strong wind knocks them off balance—I hope that it won't be soon. I often stop for lunch or coffee at a café in a small town, eavesdropping on conversations about crops, auctions, high-school sporting events, births, and deaths. It's a nice respite from my life in the city, where I am frequently held captive in an enclosed space, listening to a cell-phone fanatic engaged in a one-sided conversation.

I had the opportunity to indulge my map obsession and love of country roads when I volunteered to travel around Minnesota picking up the quilts to be included in the book *Minnesota Quilts: Creating Connections with Our Past*. The book is the result of approximately 4,000 quilt documentations completed by members of the Minnesota Quilt Project. Quilt documentation consisted of recording the history of the quilt's maker (if known), assessing age and condition of the quilt, identifying the pattern and fabrics, and taking photographs. As a coauthor of the book, I was excited by the prospect of meeting some of the quiltmakers in person and of possibly seeing more of the quilts that they had made. I gathered the quilts from their owners and drove them back to Minneapolis to be photographed. They would be returned a few days later by another volunteer. The anticipation of exploration and discovery outweighed the expected tedium of driving many miles by myself.

Once I was on the road, finding some of the homes was a challenge, as they were out in the country with no street signs or house numbers. Eventually I would find the mailbox with the correct name on it—the only way to know that I was in the right place. Many of the homes I visited had been owned by the same family for several generations and were now occupied by the family matriarch—proud, capable women who had reached three score and ten, and beyond. These old homes had many of the same characteristics; they were old, well worn, and a little frayed around the edges, but each had a unique personality, much like the quilts within.

Emma's house was far from any town, with no neighbors in sight. The house rested in the middle of a large grassy lot, with a small red barn behind it. The shrubs and trees surrounding the house seemed to protect and support it. Emma, with the help of a walker, came to the door. (I was reminded on this trip that in the country the back door is *the* door.) Emma led me through the kitchen and into the formal dining room, which was filled with dark, carved furniture from a much earlier era. My eyes surveyed the room, trying to take in the myriad items and photos that defined this family's past.

Emma's quilt—the quilt I would be taking to be photographed—was folded on the table. With modest pride, she opened the quilt to reveal a Triple Irish Chain design. It was beautifully made out of colorful scraps, many of which were feed sacks. She explained that there were almost 5,000 one-inch squares in the quilt. With remarkable memory, she told me about the fabrics that made up the quilt and where many of them came from. One of the fabrics was from a dress that Emma had made to wear to the 1933 Chicago

World's Fair. Emma had made the quilt during the Depression, when quilting bees were still a way to socialize, be productive, and be thrifty. She said that the only problem with quilting bees was that some of the quilters made stitches that were too long. Emma explained that she and her mother often would rip them out later and re-stitch them. (I heard this comment more than once.) She spoke of her children and her friends, unknowingly reassuring me that she wasn't as isolated as I'd imagined. Too soon, I had to leave to pick up another quilt.

In contrast to the quiet, country homes, one of my stops was at a home along a busy highway that carried edgy urbanites to their "up north" cabins. To accommodate the increasing volume of traffic, the highway was undergoing major construction. I looked and looked for the house, which I knew was green. I thought it would be easy to find because I had a real address with a house number and a street name! But the street signs had been taken down during construction, so I drove past the house several times before I realized it was the one I was looking for.

The little green house stood in the midst of a large, sun-scorched yard, right next to the highway project. It seemed to tremble as the huge machines bounced and rumbled past to build the new road. I pulled into the long, gravel driveway that ended in a little circle, planted with a few flowers that struggled to survive the heat. Anna came out to meet me, and led me through an enclosed porch, through the kitchen, and into her living room. As I passed through each room I seemed to step back several decades. Anna had lived in the house for more than sixty years. It originally belonged to her father; she and her baby moved in with him when her husband died at a very young age. As we talked about quilting, I looked around at the well-worn, old furnishings and I realized that keeping things as they were was probably very comfortable and comforting. Anna brought out her quilt and showed me the mail-order pattern that she had used. The pattern came from the Comfort Company in Augusta, Maine, and it included the envelope in which it had arrived, bearing a six-cent postage stamp. The name of the quilt pattern was Hexagon Star.

Anna's quilt was made in the 1940s with scraps from her and her mother's dresses, plus scraps that she got from friends. One of the fabrics, a solid green, was ordered from the Montgomery Ward catalog. Anna handpieced the many triangles and hexagons, and hand-appliquéd leaves on the "bouquets." The quilt showed signs of little, if any, use. I got the impression that it was one of the more challenging quilts that she had ever made and that she had taken good care of it.

As I prepared to leave, Anna asked me to stay for tea. Everything was ready, she said—how could I refuse? She told me about her many friends and activities. She is active in her local quilt guild and attends as many meetings as she can. The quilts that Anna makes now are usually simple, yarn-tied quilts, given to local charities for people in need. She also makes and sells rag rugs, and friends stop by regularly to buy rugs or drop off old fabric to be made into rugs. Again I was glad to hear that she wasn't always alone.

My meetings with Anna and Emma were similar to several others I had as I drove around the state. The quilters I met were always cordial and welcoming as they invited me into their homes. Talk of fabric scraps, patterns, and colors often led to reminiscing about when and why a quilt was made, and sometimes led to recalling family events that were going on at the time. I regretted that I didn't have more time to spend with each of these quilters. I would have liked to have asked them what influenced their choices of pattern and fabric in the quilts they made. Were they satisfied with how their quilts turned out? Did they enjoy the creative process, or was making the quilt just something that needed to be done?

In the months that have passed since I visited these quilters, I have thought about the impression they made on me. As women who quilt, we had a connection that allowed us to communicate immediately about one very important aspect of our lives. The quilters I met on my road trip and my quilting friends at home have vastly different personalities, and I have often marveled at how I share such a strong interest in quilting with some people with whom I have so little else in common. Much has been written about quilts as a necessity—made to keep people warm (true)—and about quilting bees as a community and a social activity where people gossip, discuss, advise, and comfort (also true). But I think that the key connection among quilters isn't the necessity of the quilt, or the social aspect of quilting, it is the gratification and pleasure of *creating* a quilt.

Quilters understand the anticipation of starting a new quilt. It might be an instantaneous decision made when a quilter sees a sample quilt in a quilt shop or a picture in a magazine. Or it may be the result of a design in progress, an idea that has resided in that patch of brain cells reserved for all thoughts quilting. Wherever it comes from, the compelling urge to create a quilt propels the quilter to her favorite source for fabric. Touching the fabric and looking at the colors is both invigorating and soothing. Watching as the fabric is unrolled from the bolt, measured, and cut represents a commitment to the idea, if not to actually completing the quilt. With fabric in hand, the creative urge has been satisfied . . . at least until next week.

Chapter Four

ALL IN THE FAMILY

"Quilts are rituals of life. Along with shelter, the quilt safeguards the human body during its greatest vulner-ability, sleep. The complex ritual of the quilt was integral to rural and frontier American survival. . . . Quilts also signaled procreation and nurture; a quilt's presence in a home, even today, tells of a family, of loved ones protected."

—William Arnett and Paul Arnett, *Gee's Bend: The Women and Their Quilts*, 2002

THROUGHOUT HISTORY, QUILTING HAS BEEN an art typically passed down from one generation to the next. In quilting families, young children learned to thread needles for the quilters long before they were allowed to take a place around the frame and add their own stitches to the quilt. As the children grew older, a mother, grandmother, or aunt taught them to sew on sampler projects, which they would use for practice until they were deemed skillful enough to move on to the next level. And then, when the time was right, the youngest quilter would join the other quilters around the frame and begin to stitch. The essays in this chapter are all about quilting experiences with family members and the lessons learned along the way.

REMEMBERING ODIN

by Elise Schebler Roberts

In the following essay, quilter and writer Elise Schebler Roberts shares fond memories of her father-in-law, Odin, as she creates a quilt in his honor. Elise learned to sew at age nine, and she started quilting in her midtwenties. After moving to Minnesota in 2001, she traded her career in museum management to become a quilt artist and historian. Elise is finishing a doctorate in education, and is a member of FireHouse Art & Quilt, a nonprofit arts cooperative. She lives in Lakeville, Minnesota, with her husband (who is also a quilter), two children, a dog, and a gecko.

Odin, my father-in-law, wouldn't give me $1.00 for my latest quilt. That was his little joke with me. And it would be true. My latest quilt is priceless. It's a memory quilt that I made in honor of Odin for my mother-in-law. Odin died not long ago.

Odin always thought it amusing that I was a quilter. The first time I met him, he told me his quilt story. Many years ago he was asked to buy a $1.00 quilt raffle-ticket. He declined, and when asked why, he replied, "I'm not giving $1.00 for an old blanket." After telling this story, he just grinned at me. My feelings were hurt, but I later learned that he was trying to tell me how naïve he was then. Odin told me that story many times in the four years I knew him. But after that first time, he always added, "You see, I didn't know then how much a blanket was really worth." In those four years, I rarely got him to say the word quilt. It was a blanket because it covered you and kept you warm. I learned to live with it, just repeating the word "quilt" every time he said "blanket."

It is difficult to be the new daughter-in-law. All families have their habits, inside jokes, and eternal mysteries. Add to that the fact that I was forty when I married into the family, and that I came with plenty of baggage, including a child, in-laws from my previous marriage, and a very definite set of ideas regarding the way my world worked. This made my new family seem even more mystifying. We were on opposite sides of the spectrum when it came to political and religious beliefs. I was a city woman, while they came from a small town. They had eight children, most of who lived within a few hours drive, while my three siblings and my parents were scattered across the country. It was difficult to find an opening, a way into the life of this new family. Sometimes I felt as if I'd shown up at the wrong party.

The way into their lives turned out to be quilting. I always had a quilt, or six, in the works. These quilts decorate my house, leaving raveled threads on floors and furniture. Because I'm a handquilter, it always takes me just a little longer to finish my quilts, and so sooner or later I knew my father-in-law was bound to come in contact with a work-in-progress. Sometimes Odin asked specifically about a quilt I was making. Other times he'd smile at me and say, "You are just like my wife, you always stay busy." Staying busy and spending time with family were important values to him. But I don't know if he understood that I wasn't just staying busy, I was staying sane. When I remarried I didn't just get a new family, I moved to a new state far from my own family and I traded in a twenty-year career as a professional research historian for a life as an artist, writer, and stay-at-home mom. All of this was my own choice, yet this was still one of the hardest periods of my life. Quilting had seen me through difficult times before, and it was with great comfort that I embarked on it as a career.

It was not long before I learned Odin's true appreciation for my career choice. Two years after we married, my husband, a computer software development manager, lost his job when the technology bubble burst. As his unemployment stretched from weeks into months, James began to look at new careers. An artist in his own right, and a technologically savvy businessperson, he gravitated to the world of computerized long-arm machine quilting. The search for the perfect machine led him to a harsh realization. We couldn't afford it. Then Odin, a former bank manager, stepped in. He listened to the issues, looked at James's research, and helped us obtain the financing we needed. When the machine arrived, he was one of the first to come see it. He and James spent hours trying out new patterns and stitches. From that point on, the first thing he'd ask us was how the quilts were going.

The last time I saw Odin was June 2004. He, my mother-in-law, and her sister went with us to the Minnesota Quilt Show in Rochester. He had not felt well for several months, but we had invited them and I think he was very curious about what he might see. This was the first time he had truly entered my world, and he was astonished at its depth. As we went through the halls, I saw his fatherly support turn to true appreciation for the art, the lives, and the ways of the quilter. He shook his head and repeated, "Just amazing!" He questioned us about technique and about fabrics. He stopped before the 9-11 quilts, and for a moment I thought he might cry. I had to keep reminding him not to touch the quilts. He put his hands behind his back and leaned in even closer. He told me the raffle-ticket story again, and this time I understood and laughed. He still called them all "blankets" and I kept reminding him to say "quilt." It was truly our first bonding experience. Eight weeks later he died of heart failure.

There is no genuine comfort you can give to someone who has lost their lifelong love. Odin and Mary had celebrated fifty-four years of marriage, and neither had regretted one day of it. Ever the caretaker, Odin had ensured that Mary was economically secure. Her eight children each used their talents and time to help her with the initial transition from coupledom to widowhood. Mary's faith provided strength and shelter in this time of uncertainty. And I felt left out. Once again I had nothing to offer.

That is, until September, when we were looking at some photos from their fiftieth wedding anniversary. I was creating memory quilts for a client, and James mentioned that I could make his mom a quilt using the anniversary photos and some of Odin's clothing. The call I made to Mary to confirm that she would indeed love a memory quilt turned out to be well timed. Mary is very efficient, and she likes to stay busy. She had already lovingly packed up Odin's clothes, and one of her children was taking them to charity. We caught them in time and diverted the boxes to our basement.

We waited a few days to open them. When we did, it was my turn to be amazed. With rare exception, I had only seen Odin in a workshirt, jeans, and a baseball cap. He even wore that cap inside the house; I'm not sure I would have recognized him without it. Expecting a box or two of clothing, I was surprised to see how many clothes he actually had. We went through boxes of dress shirts, sweaters, t-shirts, and slacks; bags of socks, shorts, and pajamas, as well as many pairs of jeans. Some of the clothes looked brand-new, while others showed signs of much-loved wear. A few of the T-shirts were obviously gifts; I saw at least one for a political candidate I had voted for but who I was pretty sure Odin didn't support. Most of the clothes were muted "guy" colors, but here and there were shades of red, yellow, green, and purple.

As we sorted through the clothes I began to discuss the quilt. My husband didn't respond. I looked up to see tears winding their way down his face. He wasn't ready for this. We packed up the boxes. A few weeks later I quietly cut up two shirts to make some test blocks. Afterward I showed them to James, hoping he could cope with it—after all, he was the one who would quilt the finished top. This time he smiled.

How do you tell a life story in a quilt? As an artist I face this question with every memory quilt I make for a client. I usually ask them to write something for me about their loved one—likes and dislikes, relationships, high and low points. We look it over, talk about color and fabric, select some blocks and I just get started.

This time I wasn't just the artist, I was also the daughter-in-law, going through my own grief and supporting a grieving husband and child. I had only known Odin four of his seventy-six years, but there were things I would miss. Like the way he was always surprised when it was me who answered the phone—I'd hear a quick breath, a little laugh, and then he'd say, "Is Jim there?" Or the projects he and my husband would plan. In his retirement, Odin had become an expert woodworker, and my laundry room has the accessories to prove it. Odin liked my eleven-year-old son from the time they met, but in the past year they had begun to develop a very special relationship. This was now at an end. My son has coped by making a shrine to his grandpa on the refrigerator. Heaven help those of us who forget this and move a photograph or a note.

Sometimes my relationship with Odin was strained—we disagreed on many political and spiritual issues. As the newest member of the family, I was often uncertain about his motivation, and my feelings were often hurt when they shouldn't have been. So how could I take this emotional package, blend it with my professional training as a historian and my love of fabric, color, and pattern, to create a quilt? I was surprised by my reluctance and my seeming inability to begin this quilt. It gave a whole new meaning to the term "Quilt Block."

When I have writer's block, I have a routine that I follow to get the words flowing again. I start with my signature. I deliberately write or type my full name in large letters. Usually the words flow quickly after that, but occasionally my name sits alone on the page, begging for some company. I decided to try the same thing with the quilt. My "signature block" is the friendship star. It's the first block I teach in beginning quilting classes. It's more complex than the basic nine-patch, and it gives new quilters a sense of accomplishment; yet no matter what fabrics or colors they pick, I've never seen it turn out badly. A twelve-inch friendship star was the perfect way to get over my Quilt Block. I found two familiar shirts: one a dusty blue with printed pockets and the other blue and white striped. I measured the shirts just to be sure the star would fit. This was just procrastination—of course I could get a twelve-inch block out of two adult shirts. I picked up my rotary cutter and made the first pass. Apparently I'd been holding my breath, because I let out a great sigh after that first cut. The worst was over; in a few minutes I'd cut my patches, one square and four triangles for the star from the blue shirt, and four squares and four triangles for the background from the striped shirt. I'd even been able to cut the star triangle from the printed shirt pocket, adding a little visual interest to the block. Now I could sew it together, and I was finally ready to plan this quilt.

I thought about the many roles Odin played in his life. He was a loving husband, a supportive father, a good friend, and a helpful community member. I love the names of quilt blocks, and I always use them to tell life stories.

First and foremost in Odin's life was his wife Mary. Their romance began as young teens, when Odin accidentally ran into her with a bicycle he was returning to her older brother. Later Mary would say when she met him that he truly knocked her off her feet. They shared many adventures working in the same hotel with her brother and sister, and by the time she was twenty they were engaged. Odin was a plainspoken and practical man, and he didn't like to waste time. After he died, Mary described his marriage proposal. One night when he dropped her at home, he looked her in the eyes and said, "Hon, I wouldn't half mind having you for a wife." Mary ran into the house, woke her parents, and told them she was engaged. She and Odin were married before her twenty-first birthday.

Odin was the center of Mary's life, so I chose to represent that with the Mary's Star quilt block. He also was her greatest admirer. The choice here was easy— I used the block Mary's Fan. The first time I met them was at their fiftieth wedding anniversary. I watched them celebrate, and I witnessed the genuine love they had for each other, undimmed, but instead strengthened, by fifty years together.

One other block was needed to honor their relationship. I chose the Lover's Knot. I will make that block from the purple shirt. Why? Because it embodies the story that perhaps best describes their ability to live with each other. One Sunday, Odin put on the purple shirt to attend church. Uncertain about which tie to wear, he picked one and asked Mary if it matched. "No," she said, "pick something else." He went back into his closet and tried on another tie. He turned to her and got the same answer. A third time he went into the closet, selected another tie, and was told once again to pick something else. Odin disappeared into the closet. He was gone a little longer this time. For a fourth time he asked Mary if his tie matched his shirt. Mary had to agree this time, as he'd selected a different shirt. Odin was practical; if they couldn't come to agreement, he was going to compromise. I actually don't know if he ever wore the purple shirt; it looked pretty new. But it and the story will live on in the center of the quilt.

In an era of smaller families, Odin was the father of eight children—four girls and four boys. There was no question that the quilt had to include an Eight Hands Around block. Sibling rivalry in a large family is intense, and this family was no exception, but Odin and Mary kept the focus on togetherness. When someone needed help, when someone had a joy or fear, the family pulled together. Each brother and sister extended a helping hand. In the four years I knew Odin, all eight siblings had been together on at least five occasions. Each had his or her own talents and weaknesses. And each stepped in accordingly. Odin raised his children gently, yet with strong expectations for behavior. He was not a man to raise his voice; however, each of the children dreaded the words "Come into my office and close the door." They knew then that they had disappointed him. No one has ever told me exactly what was said in that room, but afterward, behavior changed. Odin greatly valued being a parent.

When my husband proposed to me, he also asked to adopt my seven-year-old son, legally becoming his father as well as emotionally. James still treasures an e-mail he received right after our engagement. In it, Odin congratulates us and writes a long letter to James supporting his choice to become a parent. He reassures James that he is already a good father to my son, and that he will continue to grow in this role. The memory quilt will include a Father's Choice block.

Odin saw each of his children as individuals, so I have selected one block to represent each of his children. A plane for my husband, with whom he shared a love of flying; a golf ball for the son with whom he golfed; blocks that have the same names as some of the children; and the T-shirts that say "World's Greatest Grandpa." There were sixteen grandchildren and four great-grandchildren at the time Odin died. He was anticipating the arrival of another grandchild—the daughter James and I were adopting. Although she will only know him through photos and stories, she is a grandchild of his heart.

I started the quilt with a Friendship Star block. I will border the quilt with a constellation of Friendship Star blocks. Odin was a good friend. And all of his friends agreed that he could work a room. Strangers were just potential friends. At Odin and Mary's fiftieth anniversary, I was surprised to see so many friends from his childhood, some of whom had traveled more than 1,000 miles for the event. Odin's friends appreciated his dry wit and sincerity. Whether taking a trip with his motorcycle club or playing his weekly game of cribbage at the local coffee shop, Odin gathered a crowd. To honor their friend, his motorcycle club created a patch they wear on their jackets. It features a wolf for the club and words in his memory. Not only does each club member sport it, but they gave Mary and each of Odin's children a patch, extending the friendship to the next generation. Of course I will stitch a patch into the border.

Even Odin's business associates became his friends. At his funeral, one long-time friend shared this story. Many years ago he applied for a loan at Odin's bank. Odin was the loan officer, and while they were filling out the paperwork, the man mentioned that he was going to quit smoking. Odin finished the papers, got up, and shut the door. He looked the man in the eyes and asked if he was serious about quitting. The man squirmed a little bit, but he discussed the real challenges of quitting. Today he credits Odin for his successful break from cigarettes, and he told us, "Odin wasn't just my banker, he was a true friend."

Finally, my father-in-law was a good member of the community. He had a keen sense of right and wrong and he treated people with integrity and respect. As a young hotel clerk of color in the 1950s Midwest, Odin often faced discrimination. Many hotels would not accept people of color or people of certain religions. Odin was known in his community as someone who would defy these conventions, making a clean and safe place available to all people. The quilt will include the *Kansas City Star* block Fair and Square.

Next to his family and friends, Odin valued his faith and religion. Faith was a lifelong journey for him, taking him to different churches; he ultimately settled into a church just a few blocks from his home. Odin did nothing by halves. He was one of the first members of the national Christian Motorcycle Association. When he attended Bible study, he read the passages carefully for content and intent. For many years he taught men's group seminars with his best friend. Sometimes his religious beliefs came into conflict with my own, but I respected his passion for and his dedication to his beliefs. He was not afraid to cast a critical eye on his church, however, often writing little notes on the pastor's sermons, and delivering his recommendations after the service. It became an expected part of each Sunday that, upon leaving church, Odin would slip a piece of paper into the minister's hand, with the comment that here was something to think about. In his final hours Odin told his wife that the two things that sustained him were her and his faith. I will make a Cross and Crown block. I think I'll use the purple shirt again.

The quilt is supposed to be finished for the first anniversary of Odin's death. I don't know if I'll make it. There is so much of his life to share, so many stories to tell, so many fabrics to include. What started out as a wall hanging is now a king-sized quilt, to represent a life lived in a king-sized way. Come to think of it, maybe Odin would give me $1.00 for it, but I'd hold out for $5.00.

MY GRANDMOTHER'S LEGACY

by Patricia Cox

Lucky is the young girl with a grandmother well versed in the needle arts and eager to teach these valuable skills to her granddaughters! In "My Grandmother's Legacy," Patricia Cox reminisces about those hot summer days at the lake, when she learned to embroider at her grandmother's knee. That love of needlework eventually evolved into a love of quiltmaking. Patricia is a quilter, designer, teacher, quilt judge, lecturer, researcher, and author. She has been quilting for more than thirty-five years and has a collection of antique quilts as well as quilts she's made herself.

M y grandmother was a beautiful and strong-willed lady. Her name was Montzila Beaumont and she was half Scottish and half French. She had snapping dark brown eyes that looked almost black. She and my grandfather lived in

St. Louis, which is sometimes more Southern in attitude than parts of the Deep South. She had one sister named Helen who we never called anything but "Aunt," and Aunt's husband went by "Unc." Grandma believed in gracious living and it was fortunate that she married a moneymaker who was able to accommodate her desires. He always called her "Babe" and he managed to provide a living for Aunt and Unc, as well as a few other relatives.

There was always help in the house, and when my grandparents came up to Minnesota in the summer, Anita always came with them to do the cooking. She was probably the first black person I knew, and she did not take any nonsense from any of the grandchildren.

My mother had married a country doctor. He loved fishing as much as my grandfather, so we originally rented cabins on Lake Lizzie. Eventually the family bought property on the lake and built houses next to each other. It was here that we spent the summers. Grandpa and Grandma usually came for a month, and my mother's sisters came with their families for various periods of time to stay in my grandparent's house. My father spent the weekends at the lake. During the week he drove over every night, returning in the morning for rounds at the hospital. He and my grandfather spent a great deal of time fishing—for walleye in the evening and bass in the early morning. As kids we caught many frogs as bait for the fishermen.

Grandma always felt we should be doing something worthwhile so she brought myriad sewing projects with her. I was started on handhemming linen dishtowels and progressed through various types of needlework as my proficiency grew. There was much embroidery: black work, cut work, Swedish weaving, red work, fancy floral designs on various items, etc. Fine handsewing was also an important skill. As far as I know, my grandmother did not quilt, although one year she brought my mother a Pansy kit quilt, which I still have and which was never finished. My mother did make me a baby quilt from a kit that was probably sent to her by my grandmother. Quilting, however, was not a technique we pursued during those summer days.

So when I got married it was such a surprise to receive a quilt as a wedding present from my grandmother. It was a typical scrap 1930s Dresden Plate with blue cashing and blue centers in the plates. It also had an ice cream cone scrap border with scalloped edges all around. The quilt was one of quite a few that Grandma had purchased from the sewing circle at her church, which sold quilts to make money for various charities and missionary work.

I loved that quilt. After fifteen years of daily use in a house with four children and several dogs and quite a number of washings, it was faded and worn in places. Nobody had given me any clue as to how to care for a quilt, so it was a shock when my mother scolded me about not taking proper care of it. Love alone does not provide enough security for textiles. Fortunately for me, my grandmother had not made the quilt. The guilt would have been so much worse if that had been the case.

Needless to say, I was guilt-ridden and bewildered, wondering how to replace the cherished quilt. Grandma and Aunt were dead, and although my Mother had inherited quilts from them, she was not about to trust me with one.

My husband and I were now living in Minneapolis and we were using a cabin in Wisconsin he had inherited from his mother as a summer vacation place. As we traveled back and forth, we would stop in some of the small towns and I would place an ad in the town newspaper asking for information about any quilters in the area. This was in the mid 1960s and I received about four replies. I felt lucky to have any. One of them was from an eighty-year-old woman in Augusta, Wisconsin. On our next pass through the area, I stopped to talk to her. She had very poor eyesight but was still quilting after more than sixty years. I spent time watching her and learning about the process of making quilts. She made about six quilts for me, which I used in the cabin at the lake. But she was accustomed to using every little scrap and she pieced pieces. When she finished the quilt she would return a yard or more of fabric. I decided that I did not have to be quite so frugal, and although I appreciated all that she had shown me, I wanted to try to make a quilt on my own. My first quilt was a red, white, and blue Variable Star. I still have a picture of it, but the quilt itself was lost during one of our moves.

It was around this same time that I became involved with a group called the Pinocchio Chapter in the Kenwood area of South Minneapolis. As part of the fundraising effort to build a children's hospital in the city, the Pinocchio Chapter decorated one of the many beautiful old homes in the Kenwood area and opened it for tours during the Christmas season. We did our best to decorate it in a fitting manner. Many of the younger members of the group had never learned the needle arts, so my experience came in handy, and I found myself teaching many techniques. We also wrote instructions for making the items we used to decorate the house. There was a silent auction for the handicrafts we had made, and on the final day the house was open to the public, these handicrafts were given to the winners.

This was a wonderful experience for me, and the Christmas fundraiser was an annual event for several years. In 1969, when someone suggested that we make a quilt for one of the beds in the next Christmas House, I volunteered to make one of the blocks. We used the quilt-as-you-go method and the quilt was assembled by one of the members whose mother was a quilter. It was very successful and it made quite a bit of money. Consequently, we made another quilt the next year.

In the early 1970s I was asked to teach quilting classes to various groups. In the push to do something for the bicentennial in 1976, many women were interested in taking up quilting. I designed a Star Sampler and taught my classes how to make it.

A small ad appeared in the local newspaper at this time, asking if those interested in quilting would like to get together. Jeannie Spears headed the group, which met at the YWCA in St. Paul. Most of us who came to the meeting were quilt teachers, but it was the first time we had met one another. We came from all over the Twin Cities, and as we met we gradually got to know each other.

In 1976 six of us drove in Jeannie's camper to Detroit, Michigan, to see the National Bicentennial Quilt Show. It was exciting for us to see so many quilts all in one place. At that show I purchased my first antique quilt, from Merry Silber. It was an 1860s Feathered Star. I just could not resist it, even though I could ill afford the price.

Many more quilt conventions and symposia followed. At first the group was able to go to most of them, even though attending meant traveling all over the country, from California to Washington, D.C. I had begun designing appliqué quilt patterns and was able to make enough money to pay my way. I had such a wonderful time at each show, meeting and talking to other quilters. Everyone seemed to bubble over with pent up enthusiasm. Here were compatriots who did not look at you as if you were out of your mind when you said you were a quilter. Back in Minnesota we organized a Quilter's Retreat in order to spread our enthusiasm to the farm wives who could not afford to go to the quilt conventions. And we started a statewide organization called the Minnesota Quilters. When we hosted our first show in January 1979, we had twenty members. By the end of the show we had two hundred members. The organization has grown steadily through the years, providing a showcase for our members as well as documenting the antique quilts in the state.

Quilting has given me a chance to express my creativity. The quilts I have made and the patterns I have designed have allowed me to teach and to travel all over the world. Along the way I have amassed a collection of antique quilts. The lure of old quilts is not easy to explain or to describe to those who are not collectors. My children ask me why I want these old things when I am making new ones. There is no good answer to that question. I respect the labor and creativity of the early quiltmakers. Their ability to create such beautiful quilts with limited resources still fascinates me. I also want these quilts to have a home with someone who cares about them.

My collection was originally a teaching tool, because when I started teaching, many of my students had never seen a quilt or such a variety of them. The collection, which ranges from the early 1800s to the present, has grown over the years as I've acquired new quilts and as I've received some as gifts from those who no longer want to keep their quilts but who care enough to find a refuge for them. There are at least a dozen Dresden Plate quilts in the collection. Wherever I see one I can afford, it comes home with me. My old guilt trip is still with me, but I have never seemed able to make one myself, although I do have four cut out and sitting in my sewing room, waiting for that magical moment when I assemble them and bring them to life.

Quilting has been my salvation though these past forty years. It has kept me going through good and bad times and it has given me a wealth of experience. Little did my grandmother know that her needlework lessons and her wedding gift would make such a difference in my life. I think of her often and of the legacy she left me.

EXCERPT FROM *GEE'S BEND: THE WOMEN AND THEIR QUILTS*

by Belinda Pettway

In Gee's Bend, Alabama, quiltmaking has been a part of everyday life for generations. In this tiny town that was long isolated from surrounding communities by a bend in the Alabama River, quiltmakers without the means to buy new fabric began to make quilts from the remnants of old work clothes. In 2003, Tinwood Media gathered a number of the quilts for an exhibition that would appear in art museums around the United States. In addition to the exhibition, Tinwood Media produced a book, *Gee's Bend: The Women and Their Quilts*, which features all of the quilts on display plus many more, with stories about the quilts, their makers, and Gee's Bend itself. The stories are sometimes lighthearted, sometimes heartwrenching, but always fascinating. The following story is told by Belinda Pettway, a quiltmaker who, like many in Gee's Bend, comes from a long line of quilters.

I was born in 1957, down there where my mother stay. They call it John Pettway Road now, after my daddy. They call that part Sodom, been calling it that ever since I know myself. Most of all, when I was little I just did what all the other children used to do: pick cotton, cucumbers, squashes. My daddy sold them at the place up by the store where they sold them at. A man named Roman Pettway used to buy them and then he take them and sell them.

We used to go to school from August to May. I finished twelfth grade at Pine Hill High School. I liked math but didn't care much for stuff like English and social studies. I like to do problems. I like to solve them. I was sewing quilts back when I was going to school. My mama just started learning me how to sew and I started sewing. I just started cutting pieces and sewing them together. I never did like looking at no books, no patterns. Just cut them out and sew them. I could see other people sewing from patterns but I never did like a pattern. I liked to be on my own. I never even liked to make two of them alike. I wanted them different. I just lay the pieces out on the floor or on the bed until I get enough, until I get them straight. Like, I cut them out and put them together, and I start with one or two pieces, and when they look right I sew them together. Then I get another piece and sew it onto that. Keep going on until it looks right and it's the right size for the bed. If it doesn't look right to me, I take it a-loose and put something else in until it do look right. It's like doing the problem in school. You get two pieces here and two there and you got to make it come out to four, four pieces that suit you. You can't just put a quilt together any kind of a way; you got to make the pieces fit to suit you. When I look at it, I'll know when it's right.

I married Lonnie Lee Pettway in 1980. Me and him raised six children, two girls and four boys. My mother, Annie Bell, raised my oldest, a boy I had before I married Lonnie Lee. Quilts have been in my family on all sides. My mama, my mama's mama—Cherokee—and her sisters Clementine and Nell, and my daddy's mama, all of them made quilts. My husband and me live right behind his grandmother's house. She is Martha Jane Pettway. She was a very good quilter. So was Lonnie Lee's mother, Joanna. She was one of my main teachers until she passed in '97. She was caring for Martha Jane and after she passed, Martha Jane moved down to Mobile. She lives there now, 102 years old. Martha Jane was still piecing up quilts right up to when Joanna passed. Didn't want to go to Mobile but didn't have no other choice.

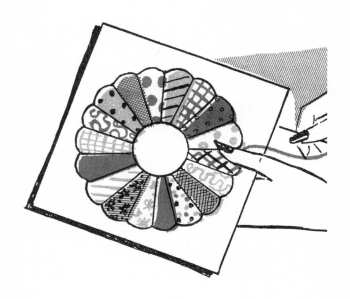

Chapter Five

AROUND
THE QUILT FRAME

"Haying and threshing and clover-seed hulling
and road-work day belonged to the men. But
quilting day belonged to the women. It was
alright for a man to deliver his wife at a quilting,
but he had to get away as fast as he could. If he
went to the house and sat down with the women-
folks and tried to be sociable, they'd have him
run out with brooms."

—Homer Croy, *Country Cured,* 1943

QUILTS ADDED COMFORT AND BEAUTY to a home, but they served another purpose as well. With so much work to be done, there was seldom time to visit with friends and family. But when a quilt was pieced and ready to be quilted, friends and neighbors would gather to sit around the quilt frame and help stitch. These quilting bees were ideal for getting a lot of work done at once—a group would often complete more than one quilt in a sitting—and, best of all, the women were able to socialize while they stitched. The quilters would usually stay all day, breaking every few hours for coffee or a snack. Women with children would often bring them along to play while the women worked and talked. At the end of the day, husbands would come in from the fields, sometimes joining the quilters for a potluck dinner. After the dishes were cleared, one of the men might play a few songs on his fiddle. At some homes, quilt frames could actually be hoisted to the ceiling, allowing room for couples to dance! Although there's no dancing in the following stories about quilting bees, it's clear that the friends women made through quilting were cherished indeed.

QUILTS IN THE LIFE CYCLE

by Rachel T. Pellman and Joanne Ranck

In the Amish and Mennonite communities, quiltings are much anticipated social events. Authors Rachel T. Pellman and Joanne Ranck describe the importance of quilting in Amish society in their book *Quilts among the Plain People*, published by Good Books in 1981. Both women are quilters who were raised in Lancaster County, Pennsylvania, and who graduated from Eastern Mennonite College.

F arm and rural life is organized around the work flow of the seasons. So is sewing. Many women find time to quilt during long winter evenings when the family is gathered indoors and the snow blows outside. It is a relaxing pastime but also worthwhile. In the spring and summer, gardening and food preservation take priority; quilting projects are laid aside.

As life has its stages, so do quilts. At a very young age children may be taught the basics of sewing quilt patches.

As they grow older fewer boys participate; sewing becomes women's work. A girl feels a sense of pride in being allowed to help stitch a quilt in her mother's frame. It identifies her with grown-up women. And to be allowed to quilt rather than help get lunch at a quilting bee is a statement about one's aptitude in quilting.

Young people generally marry in their late teens and early twenties. A woman's responsibilities then include housekeeping, gardening, and often sewing for the family. Although there are usually stores in areas with a sizeable population of plain folk which stock plain clothing for men, women's cape dresses are almost always homemade. Sewing leaves a woman with a whole collection of fabric ends and snippets. Frugally she will store them, accumulating a collection from which a scrap quilt can be made.

When a young woman goes to housekeeping she is expected to have anywhere from two to thirteen quilts completed and ready for use. At the time of marriage it is not unusual for a girl to receive four to six quilts as a gift from her mother. These will be enough for her to begin her home and use until she is established and has daughters of her own who can help quilt.

Children are seen as a gift from God and are treated as such. Frequently a woman will make a crib quilt in joyful anticipation of a child. Children are disciplined at an early age but not with harshness. It is the parents' desire that their children do right that inspires their strong but loving training.

Women are always worthwhile. Roles are clearly defined and both male and female duties are viewed with dignity. Many a man will quietly boast of his wife's knack with a needle. Some responsibilities are shared. A woman will work the fields if necessary. Little girls as well as little boys learn to plow.

How do these women with large families, houses, and gardens find time to quilt?

Time is a relative thing. In the Old Order society, extended families are common. Three generations live and work on the same homestead. That fact eases life a great deal. If grandmother is too feeble to work outdoors she can still lead a rich and full life helping to entertain children or make quilts indoors. Non-physical labor is often done by the elderly folks.

It would be misleading to say that all women in Amish and Mennonite communities quilt. For some, quilting is as natural as housecleaning and gardening. For others, it is tedious work and something they simply prefer not doing. Some women in professional fields know little about sewing or do not have time for it.

A QUILTING

Among a people who shy away from TV, radio, movies, and much entertainment experienced by the larger society, visiting is vital. Visiting happens among family and relatives. It includes friends and neighbors who may drop by for the Sunday noon meal and afternoon; it may be an evening with no purpose other than enjoying the company of another family.

A quilting bee is an all-day visit for a group of women who get together to finish a quilt top. Quiltings may be held anytime, although they occur much more frequently from late fall through early spring.

There is no regular pattern as to how often quiltings are held. A woman will call family and friends together when she has a top ready to be done.

Is It Work or Pleasure?

A typical quilting in a home usually involves between eight and sixteen women. They arrive in the morning after the school-age children are given a proper breakfast and sent on their way. Preschoolers come along and with a number of friends enjoy the day as much as their mothers. Children may be asked to keep a supply of threaded needles on hand.

Upon arriving, the women are ready to begin work. If the quilt to be completed is not already in the frame, those coming first will help to stretch it and put it in. Each woman then takes her place around the frame and quilting begins.

It may take a while to be seated. There is good-natured jesting about where to sit. No one wants to be next to the fastest quilter because she will be ready to "roll" before they are. Straight lines are easier to quilt than curves so the less experienced quilters will sit at those places if they exist.

A large frame is used, allowing the surface of the quilt to be stretched fully open at the start of a bee. Quilting begins around all four sides. Each woman quilts the area in front of her, reaching as far toward the center as she comfortably can. When she can no longer reach, the quilt is ready to be rolled. The two long wooden poles to which the sides of the quilt have been pinned or basted are released from their clamps and the completed part is gently rolled under, bringing the distant section close to the edge. The quilt is pulled taut and quilting begins again from the edge. The women follow light pencil lines which create the decorative quilting pattern, with tiny stitches, each one reaching through to connect all three layers of the quilt.

The woman hosting the quilting is in charge of the day, seeing that things run smoothly. She also provides a hearty dinner at noon in exchange for the help with her quilt. The meal is remuneration, and it provides an easy and acceptable "out" for women who either should not (because of their less than standard workmanship) or would rather not quilt. These women are given kitchen duty and enjoy it fully.

Being assigned to the kitchen when you would rather quilt can be humbling. It is sometimes the younger girls whose stitches are not yet tiny or neat enough who get that job. To be invited to quilt in a quilting at a young age is an honor.

Conversation around lunch and the quilt frame is jovial and, to say the least, enlightening. It is the place to catch up on all the latest news, household tips, garden hints, home remedies, childrearing information, weather, marriage, births, and deaths. Conversations become more intimate as the quilt gets smaller and women come closer together. By early afternoon a top can be completed.

EXCERPT FROM
THE PERSIAN PICKLE CLUB

by Sandra Dallas

Sandra Dallas has been a quilter for more than thirty-five years, and today she is an avid collector of antique quilts. She lives in Denver, Colorado, and is the author of *The Quilt That Walked to Golden*, *Buster's Midnight Café*, *Alice's Tulips*, and *The Persian Pickle Club*, from which this piece was excerpted. The story, which takes place in Harveyville, Kansas, during the 1930s, chronicles the friendships that develop among a group of quilters who call themselves the Persian Pickle Club. The following excerpt is heavily laced with town gossip. The Persian Pickles are meeting for the first time after members Queenie Bean and Rita Ritter are stopped late one night on a deserted country road and attacked by a vagrant. Just before the incident occurred, the two had been out interviewing townsfolk about a murder and they suspect their attacker may have had something to do with the crime. And as the Pickles add stitches to a celebrity quilt they made to be auctioned off for charity, they put their heads together to save the reputation of a member's daughter who has fallen on hard times.

I wasn't like Rita. I couldn't go running all over the county talking to people the way she did—not after what happened to us. I was ashamed to show my face.

So Tom borrowed the Ritters' car, and he drove her instead. I know she was disappointed in me, but the farm was the only place I felt safe, and I refused to leave it, even to be with my best friends. I called Forest Ann to say I wouldn't attend the Persian Pickle Club, which was at her house that day.

Mrs. Judd stopped by for me, anyway. I heard her turn off the motor of the Packard and coast to a stop by my back steps, and I went to the kitchen door to see who it was. Ella peered over the big dashboard and fluttered her hand at me.

Mrs. Judd was already halfway up the stairs when I reached the door. Each step creaked in turn as she put her weight on it. She stopped at the door, breathing hard, the sweat on her face making her warts shine like little steel tacks. "I didn't know if you were feeling up to driving to Pickle this afternoon. Ella and I came to fetch you," she said to me through the screen. Old Bob got up off the floor and peered out at her, then wagged his tail. He was good company, but he wasn't much of a watchdog.

"I'm not going today," I told her. "Thank you just the same."

"Yes you are," Mrs. Judd said as she yanked at the screen door. It didn't open because I'd begun putting the hook on when Grover wasn't in the house. "Thunderation! You're living like a crow in a cage. Open this door."

I wanted to tell her it was none of her business if I locked up my house. Instead, I said, "I have a headache. I'm not going."

"You've never had a headache in your life, Queenie Bean. Now unlatch this screen." Mrs. Judd folded back the veil on her hat and pushed up her sleeves, ready to yank the door off the hinges if I didn't mind her. So I reached up and lifted the hook, and Mrs. Judd stepped inside. She was still puffing, not just from the exertion of climbing the stairs but from the strain of looking after Ella the past weeks. Ella had gotten even more childlike, and I wondered if she might live with the Judds forever.

Mrs. Judd settled herself on a kitchen chair, intending to stay there until she'd spoken her mind. "Now, Queenie, I know you've had a hard time of it. I'm not saying you haven't. But there're others less

fortunate than you. You don't know the half of it."
She stopped a minute and frowned, as if she'd said
too much.

"You can stay locked up here feeling sorry for
yourself like Lizzy Olive would have done, or you can
put the bad time behind you like Ella did and think
about all the good things the Lord gave you. And
He'll keep on giving them to you if you'll let Him. But
how can you take advantage of His opportunities if
you're sitting behind the kitchen door with the hook
on?" Mrs. Judd took a breath and leaned forward,
resting her forearms on her thighs.

"Here's another thing. Forest Ann's already set in
the Celebrity Quilt, and we're going to start stitching
on it this afternoon. You ought to be there, because
we're all so excited about it that we might stay and
finish it up by evening, and wouldn't that be a shame
if you didn't get one stitch on it? So you go put on
that orchid dress with the yellow rickrack that makes
you look so sweet, and then we'll be on our way." Mrs.
Judd shifted her weight, putting a strain on the chair,
whose joints squeaked in protest. "You got any of
Ceres's burnt-sugar cake left for us to sample? I'll get it
out of the fridge myself. Ella needs something that'll

stick to her bones." As she got up to rummage through my refrigerator, she called through the door, "Ella, sugar pie, Queenie wants you to come on in here for refreshments while we wait."

The Celebrity Quilt changed my mind about attending Persian Pickle. I felt more comfortable going now that someone else would take me, because I was afraid that if I got behind the wheel of the Studebaker, I'd shake too much to drive. So I changed my dress and brushed my hair, and by the time I was ready, Ella and Mrs. Judd were rinsing off their plates in the sink. Grover came out of the barn as I got into the Packard. When I told him I was going to club after all, he just nodded, as if he'd expected me to. He and Mrs. Judd actually might have cooked this up between them.

If they had, I was especially glad, since Rita was there ahead of me. I was surprised, because Rita didn't like Persian Pickle the way I did, and I'd already told her I wasn't going. So I thought she'd stay home, too.

She came skipping out of Forest Ann's house when she saw me and whispered, "I'd think driving with Mrs. Judd would be as scary as . . . you know. . . ." I laughed.

Nettie overheard and was shocked—not because we'd said something against Mrs. Judd's driving. We all made remarks about that. Nettie acted as if it was blasphemous for us to joke about what had happened to us. Of course, it would have been if our husbands had, or even the other Pickles. But the jokes were a bond between Rita and me, and making fun of that night helped us.

Rita drew me off to one side. "I had a look at the coroner's report," she whispered. "Doc Sipes wrote there wasn't a thing about Ben's body that proved he'd been murdered. For all he knew, Ben had fallen out of a tree and somebody'd put him in the ground to save the cost of a funeral. Now, why would he say a thing like that?"

I shook my head.

"Why would he unless somebody paid him to?" she asked.

"And who's the only one in Harveyville who has enough money to spend bribing a coroner?" Rita glanced in Mrs. Judd's direction.

Mrs. Judd saw us looking at her and called me to come inside to see the Celebrity Quilt, and in my excitement, I forgot about Doc Sipes and who might want to pay him to put lies in his report.

The Celebrity Quilt was beautiful. Over the summer, as the autographs had come in, we'd embroidered them in red, but we'd waited until fall to put the quilt together, just in case some of the famous people we'd written to had been on vacation and hadn't gotten their mail. Forest Ann and Mrs. Ritter assembled the embroidered squares into rows, setting off each one with borders of red cotton. Then they stitched the strips together into a quilt. Where the corners met, they added tiny red-and-white nine-patch squares. It was as fresh and as pretty a quilt as I'd ever seen. Forest Ann had set it into the wooden quilt frame in the middle of her dining room, the big oak pedestal table pushed into the corner.

I stood at the edge of the quilt and fingered Lew Ayres's autograph. Then I ran my hand over "Good Luck, Eleanor Roosevelt," thinking I'd never met a woman who could look at a piece of material without touching it. I bet even Eleanor Roosevelt had pinched that fabric between her thumb and forefinger before she wrote her name. I looked over the rows of famous names and felt pride that they were all part of a quilt in Harveyville, Kansas—a quilt that'd been my idea.

We stood impatiently, waiting for Forest Ann to assign us places around the quilt, which it was her privilege to do, since we were at her house. Ella was the best quilter, so of course she'd work on the center, where the stitches showed the most. I was surprised when Forest Ann didn't put her there. She asked Ella to sit on the side. Then she placed Rita next to Ella instead of at the lower end, where the poorest quilter usually sat. That was a nice thing to do, even though Rita didn't understand what a compliment it was.

Then Forest Ann said, "Queenie, would you sit here, please, where you can work on the center." Everyone smiled and nodded.

"Ella ought to be there," I protested.

"No, the Celebrity Quilt was your idea. You deserve the honor," she replied. "Besides, you're a fine quilter."

I blushed and sat down on one of Forest Ann's dining-room chairs. Now I knew why Mrs. Judd had made me come to Persian Pickle. She and Forest Ann had planned this ahead of time. I looked up and saw Mrs. Judd smiling at me, and I felt so lucky to have such good friends that tears came to my eyes. I didn't want anyone to see, for fear they'd think I was crying over that night, so I picked up my pocketbook and searched for my thimble. Then I threaded my needle and took a stitch, carefully pulling the knot through the quilt top to hide it, and began to make tiny stitches around Edgar Bergen's autograph.

With all the sorrows we'd been through, we hadn't had a regular Persian Pickle in the longest time. The last one, in fact, had been at Opalina's, the day that Hiawatha found Ben Crook's bones. Of course, with all the troubles, we'd seen plenty of one another, but I realized as I stitched how much I'd missed all of us sitting down and working together. There was something homey and comfortable about the way we bent over the quilt in Forest Ann's parlor. I had Grover, and I had the Persian Pickle. Some made do with a lot less.

"This sure is a pretty quilt," Mrs. Ritter said. "Don't you think so, Rita."

Rita muttered, "Uh-huh."

"Are you going to write another newspaper story about it?" Mrs. Judd asked. Rita's first story about the Celebrity Quilt had been only a paragraph, and it hadn't included any of our names.

Rita shrugged without looking up. "I'm pretty busy right now." She yanked at her needle, and the

174

thread pulled out of it. Rita licked the end of the thread, flattened it between her thumb and finger, and pushed it back through the eye of the needle.

Mrs. Judd stopped stitching to watch Rita. "Tell me why people's so crazy to read about a murder? It seems to me they'd rather read about what a body's doing for those less fortunate."

Mrs. Judd looked over at Ella, who didn't seem to be paying attention. Sometimes I wondered if Ella heard one single thing we said anymore. Her mind had always wandered, but since Ben's funeral, she seemed more than ever to be living in some place that was far off from Harveyville.

Rita looked up and gave Mrs. Judd a smug smile, as if she knew a secret she wasn't telling. "Really?"

"It would be awful nice if they ran a picture," Opalina said.

"Of us?" Ada June asked.

"Of the quilt, of course," Opalina said, but Ada June and I exchanged glances. We both knew Opalina meant of us. I thought it would be awful nice, too.

"Maybe I'll write about the quilt later on," Rita said. "Right now, I can't let Queenie down. After what happened to us, I gave her my word that I'd solve . . .

Mr. Crook's . . . you know. . . ." She glanced at Ella and didn't finish. I put my needle down, wondering if I should protest. She'd never given me her word she'd find Ben Crook's killer for my sake. Nor did I ask her to promise any such thing, but I realized the club members knew that. So I kept my mouth shut.

Ceres took a couple of backstitches and bit off her thread with her teeth, then reached for her spool. "If you ask me, it was just your bad luck you getting stopped like you did. There wasn't anybody after the two of you. The man who did it was only a bum passing through," she said. "I meant to tell you, Cheed said that he heard a car got stopped over to Emporia last evening because of a stump in the middle of the road."

Rita and I looked at each other, and Opalina asked, "What happened?"

"Nothing. Two big men got out of the car and moved the stump."

Opalina cast a sidelong glance at Ceres, waiting for her to continue. When she didn't, Opalina said, "I don't get it. If nothing happened, what does that prove?"

"Why, that's the point of it, dearie. That stump didn't just sprout by itself. Whoever's doing this doesn't

176

have any idea who'll be coming along. It was an accident that two men were in the car last evening just like it was an accident that Queenie and Rita were the ones who were stopped here. When that robber saw grown men get out of the car, he stayed hid. There's your proof."

"What I think—" Agnes T. Ritter said, but Mrs. Ritter had been watching Rita, who was getting fidgety as she listened to Ceres and Opalina. So she interrupted Agnes T. Ritter.

"I've been wondering. How many raffle tickets do you think we're going to sell on this quilt?" Mrs. Ritter asked.

Agnes T. Ritter was annoyed because she hadn't been allowed to tell us what she thought, and she opened her mouth to try again. But I didn't care what she had to say. Besides, like Rita, I didn't want to hear any more about the men in Emporia. So I piped up, "I'm going to ask Grover to sell the farm and buy all of the chances. That way, I'll win the quilt."

"My stars! To think a farm in Harveyville is worth that much," Mrs. Ritter said.

We talked about the price we'd charge for the tickets and how many we'd print and who would buy them, and before we knew it, Forest Ann called, "Ready to roll?"

"Ready," I said.

"Just hold your horses," Mrs. Judd told us. She'd tangled her thread and had to break it off. Then she cut a new length, put it through her needle, and took hurried stitches. As the rest of us completed our sections, we stood up and stretched and admired one another's stitching. We were making good time.

At last, Mrs. Judd snipped off her thread and said, "Ready to roll."

We stood back and watched while Forest Ann and Agnes T. Ritter rolled the part of the quilt we'd just stitched over the top of the frame, unrolling an unquilted section from the bottom at the same time.

While they did that, Ada June came over to me and put her arm around my waist. "I'm glad you came, Queenie. That's my favorite dress of yours," she said. I thanked her, and she whispered, "Aren't you glad Mrs. Judd forgot about reading?"

"Oh, boy, am I!" I whispered back, although I wasn't so sure Mrs. Judd had forgotten. We all felt the need to visit.

As we took our places again, I saw Forest Ann pat Nettie's arm. Nettie moved her neck as much as she could to smile up at her sister-in-law. Then her mouth trembled, and I wondered if Tyrone's rheumatism was acting up again. I hoped not. I'd rather slop pigs than have to sit through another evening of tending Tyrone Burgett in a sickbed. Nettie looked worn out, and I thought that with all her worries, she'd been an especially good friend, calling on me with a molasses pie and some of her fruitcake after what had happened to me.

"I hope those pregnant girls appreciate all the work we're doing on this quilt," Agnes T. Ritter said after we'd gone back to stitching.

"Agnes! For goodness sakes!" Mrs. Ritter looked at Agnes T. Ritter and shook her head.

"I'm just saying we went to a whole lot of work, and for all we know, it's for a bunch of tarts. That's who stays in those homes, you know. Girls with no moral sense!" She pressed her skinny lips together.

Nettie drew in her breath so sharply that we all looked up at her.

"Well, maybe not every one, but I'll bet you most of them are. You can like it or lump it. I'm just saying what I think, which is girls who get in the family way when they're not married are no more than trash." Agnes T. Ritter sure was in a bad mood that day.

Mrs. Ritter reached across the quilt and touched her arm. "Agnes, that's enough. We're not here to pass judgment."

Agnes T. Ritter put her pointy nose in the air, but she shut up.

Nettie turned her face away, but not before we saw the tears running down it. She tried to get up, but her chair was wedged in between Ella's and Opalina's, and she couldn't move. So she put her hands over her face and began to sob, the tears running down her nose and dripping on the autograph of Bebe Daniels.

Forest Ann got up and stood behind Nettie, her arms around her. "It's all right, honey. Everything's going to be all right." Forest Ann sniffed back a few tears of her own. "Nettie's just concerned about Tyrone," she told us.

But we knew Tyrone wasn't the cause of Nettie's tears. One by one, as we remembered what had set Nettie off, we put our needles down and looked at Nettie with sympathy. No, it wasn't Tyrone. Except for Ella, who never did understand what was going on, Agnes T. Ritter was the last one to get it, and when she did, she sucked in her breath and said, "Velma's . . . Velma's . . . Oh, I didn't . . . Oh my God!"

"Be still," Mrs. Judd told her quietly. "Ella, sweetheart, do you have my scissors?"

"Oh," Ella said, looking around her chair.

All of us searched about our places for the scissors until Mrs. Judd held them up in the air and said, "Good heavens, they were right here in my workbasket all the time." Of course, she'd known they were. She wanted to give Nettie a chance to blow her nose and dry her eyes with a piece of toilet paper from her pocket. By the time we turned to Nettie again, she'd stopped crying, but her eyes were red and her face was blotchy. The scarf had slipped off her neck, and her goiter quivered like a piglet. Forest Ann, who was still standing in back of Nettie's chair, tucked the scarf into Nettie's collar.

"I guess you could say Velma's one of the less fortunates," Nettie said at last, giving a short, bitter laugh.

"It's her business," Mrs. Ritter said, taking three or four stitches in the quilt and pulling the thread through. "It's not ours."

"It'll be everybody's business before long," Forest Ann said.

Mrs. Judd picked up her needle and took a stitch, and the rest of us followed. Then Rita piped up. "We used to say in college that the first baby can come anytime. After that, it takes nine months." Rita failed to notice that the rest of us didn't think it was funny. "When's Velma getting married?"

Nettie sent her a quick look. "She's not."

"Oh!" Agnes T. Ritter said. "Oh, heavens!"

"He's a married man, if you must know," Nettie said, and began crying again.

We all made little murmurs of sympathy until Mrs. Judd cleared her throat. "What does Tyrone say?"

"He doesn't know. Velma's afraid to tell him. I'm afraid to tell him, too, if you want to know the truth," Nettie said. "You know how much he sets store by how a person keeps the commandments." She looked around the circle at each one of us as if under these circumstances we'd point out that Tyrone Burgett's standards were always for the other fellow! As far as I knew, Tyrone didn't personally keep any of the commandments, apart from not working on the Sabbath.

"Nettie and Velma don't want to disappoint Tyrone. He'd be so hurt," Forest Ann put in. We all knew that wasn't it. They were afraid Tyrone would throw Velma out of the house, and maybe Nettie with her.

"Sometimes these young girls have accidents," Opalina said. We all knew exactly what Opalina meant, and I shuddered.

"No," Forest Ann said quietly. "I asked Doc Sipes. Velma's too far along. It would likely kill her."

I looked down at the quilt and saw how crooked my last few stitches were, and I pulled them out.

"I guess it's up to us to figure out what's to become of Velma," Mrs. Judd said. She was right. The others knew it and stopped talking to concentrate on sewing. We were women who turned to our needles when there were problems to be dealt with.

"If she needs a place to stay, she can always live with Cheed and me," Ceres said. "We'd welcome a young person—and a baby."

Nettie shook her head. "That wouldn't work because Tyrone would find out about it, and he'd give you 'Hail, Columbia' along with Velma and me. But thank you just the same, Ceres."

Nettie put her needle aside and said in a voice filled with shame, "Besides, Velma doesn't want to keep the baby."

"Oh," I said, wondering why women like Velma and Rita, who didn't want children, got pregnant, while God denied me a baby even though I wanted one more than anything in the world. He even gave five at one time to that Dionne family in Canada. Was that fair? Maybe things like that happened because God was a man and didn't understand. I wanted to ask the others what they thought, but I was afraid Nettie would call me blasphemous.

Nettie glanced at me and continued. "I'm not saying Velma's wrong about that, but it would break my heart knowing there's a tiny baby out there someplace who's Velma's flesh and blood, and mine, too, and it's living in an orphan home with nobody to love it. The baby will end up in one of those places, just like corn in a crib, if Velma doesn't keep it, since nobody in times like these can afford to take in an extra mouth to feed. It's not right to leave a baby to be brought up an orphan." Nettie poked her needle into the quilt and took a single stitch. "Velma'll have to stay here in Harveyville to have the baby. We don't even have the money to send her to a home. They charge something, you know."

"We could all help out," Opalina said. "We could raise the money ourselves."

"We're women. All we have is egg money. If we ask our husbands, well, we'll have to tell them why, and then everybody will know," Ada June said.

That was true. Agnes T. Ritter began to say something but stopped before Mrs. Ritter could interrupt her. The rest of us thought hard but couldn't come up with any suggestions. Finally, when it seemed like there was no answer at all, Mrs. Judd spoke up, and it occurred to me that she'd had a plan all along. "I know one person who could pay, that is if he doesn't spend all his money trying to corner the market on this quilt," Mrs. Judd said.

I looked up quickly because it sounded like she meant Grover. He and I were better off than most. That was true. But we didn't have money to throw away, and if we had, Grover wouldn't give it to Tyrone Burgett's daughter. Mrs. Judd was staring at me, and I stared right back while the others looked from her to me. Then I had a terrible thought, and before I could stop myself, I blurted out, "Are you saying Grover's the father? Are you accusing Grover of committing adultery?" I heard one of the Pickles suck in her breath, but I didn't look because I wouldn't take my eyes off Mrs. Judd.

"Oh, no such thing!" Mrs. Judd said quickly. "Don't get your dander up, Queenie. I know well

enough who Velma took up with, and so do you, I
expect. What I'm saying is this: Velma's going to have
a baby she doesn't want, and you want a baby you
don't have. Now we can use one problem to solve the
other. If Grover's willing to pay for Velma's keep in
Kansas City, I'd guess she'd let you keep the baby. Isn't
that about right, Nettie?"

"Well, I . . ."

"Oh course she would. It's a fact," Mrs. Judd
told her.

My hand holding the needle began to shake. I'd
been doing a lot of shaking lately, but this time it was-
n't from fear. I tried to stop it with my other hand, but
I jammed myself so hard with the needle that a drop
of blood ran out onto the autograph of Mae West. I
didn't feel the prick because what Mrs. Judd had said
was running around inside my mind like a chicken
without its head, and there wasn't room in there to
think of anything else. I knew the club members had
stopped talking and were staring at me, but I couldn't
make their faces come into focus.

"What if Velma wanted it back?" I asked at last.

"She doesn't. I already asked her," Mrs. Judd said.
"You and Grover'd have to adopt it legal, of course. If

Velma ever did want it back, she'd have no way to prove it was hers. Still, she won't. She's got no way to support it, and the father won't have anything to do with it—or her, either, after she told him about the baby. Why, he said it wasn't even his. Besides, you know Velma. She's wanted to get out of Harveyville since the day she was born. She says after the baby comes, she'll stay on in Kansas City or move to Chicago or Omaha, anywhere that isn't Harveyville, Kansas."

"Harveyville's not so bad," Opalina said.

"That's beside the point," Mrs. Judd told her, glancing at Opalina just long enough to let her know she thought Opalina was crazy. Opalina ducked her head and returned to her stitching. Everyone else turned to me.

"I don't know if Grover would raise a foundling," I said.

"Velma's baby's not a foundling!" Forest Ann spoke up. "It's not a pig in a poke, where you don't know if it's got an inherited disease or foreign blood. Grover will know that it came from a Christian family."

Grover would also know that it came from Tyrone Burgett's family, because I wouldn't deceive him.

Grover had no use at all for Tyrone, and he didn't approve of Velma, either, not after she'd gone to town. Still, he knew she'd been a nice girl once. Would Grover blame a baby for its mother? I didn't know.

The baby's parents weren't the only problem. There was another question, and that was: Would Grover want to raise anybody else's baby at all? We'd never talked about adopting. After Dr. Sipes told me I'd never get pregnant again, babies were a subject neither one of us ever brought up.

"Well?" Mrs. Judd asked me. All the Pickles were waiting for a reply.

I looked at her, then at Nettie, and back at Mrs. Judd. "I could ask him," I said slowly. "I'd have to tell him the truth. It wouldn't be right not to."

"Grover Bean'll do anything you say. If you ask him, it's as good as done," Mrs. Judd said. "I guess this settles it."

Nettie quivered a little and reached up to pat Forest Ann's hand, which was on her shoulder. "I won't interfere, Queenie. I promise you that. It would be your baby. But could I come visit sometimes? Would that be all right?"

"Well, of course you could! All of you can," I said. "Even Velma could come and visit."

"Oh, she wouldn't," Nettie said quickly.

The others went back to quilting, but I was too excited to continue my sewing, even if I was stitching Mae West's name. I stuck my needle into the quilt top and leaned back in my chair, shutting my eyes to recall everything that had been said. The conversation had happened so quickly that it made me dizzy. In hardly more time than it took to sew a thread length, I'd gone from a barren woman to a mother—that is, if Grover approved. But Mrs. Judd was right about that. Grover wouldn't say no. When I opened my eyes, I saw my friends glancing up at me as they quilted, and smiling. I was going to have a baby!

"When it's time for her to show, Velma'll just say she got a job in Kansas City," Mrs. Judd said, and we all nodded. "It'll be our secret, of course. Except for Grover, we won't tell a soul."

"That's crazy!" Rita blurted out. "I never heard of anything so dumb. Nobody can keep a secret like that. Someone will let it slip, and in five minutes, the whole town will know."

"No," I said.

"I'm sorry, Queenie, but somebody's going to tell."

Mrs. Judd held her needle still and peered at Rita

over her glasses. She looked down at the square in front of her and ran her hand over it before she said in a flat, even voice, "The rest of us can keep a secret. Were you planning on telling?"

"No, of course not." Rita looked uncomfortable.

Mrs. Judd shrugged. "Then that's that. There's nothing to worry about." She looked over the quilt and asked, "Ready to roll?"

We stood up and stretched, except for Rita, who stayed in her chair, shaking her head.

Persian Pickle lasted late because we stayed to finish the Celebrity Quilt, just as Mrs. Judd had predicted, even though I was in the worst hurry to get home and talk to Grover. But I'd come with Mrs. Judd, so I had to wait while we took the quilt out of the frame and held it up for everyone to admire, then turned it over to look for places we'd missed. At last, Opalina got out her Kodak and took views of all of us standing on the porch, holding the quilt.

After that, I hopped from one foot to the other, waiting for Mrs. Judd to leave, and even walked over to the Packard, hoping that would hurry her up.

The club members carried the quilt back into the house, but Rita remained outside, leaning against

Forest Ann's cistern, watching the women. She ought to have felt comfortable at Persian Pickle by now. We'd all made such an effort with her. But she still seemed to be apart from us, and I wondered if she'd ever really be a member. Rita motioned for me to come over to her.

"Queenie, you're nuts if you go along with this. I know the female sex," Rita said.

"Maybe you do, but I know these women, and they won't say anything. I trust them." I watched Mrs. Judd come down the steps with Nettie, whose legs were lumpy under her flesh-colored cotton stockings, and wondered if Velma's baby would have sawdust legs like that. The idea made me grin.

Rita thought I'd smiled because of what she'd said. "I don't know why you think that's funny. If you knew what I know, you wouldn't trust Mrs. Judd any farther than you could throw her." Now Rita smiled. "Farther than you can throw her. That's pretty funny, huh? I bet even Grover couldn't throw her more than a foot." I didn't answer. After all Mrs. Judd had just done for me, I wasn't about to make fun of her.

Rita pushed out her lower lip when I didn't reply, then tossed her head back, sending her buttery curls bouncing. "I've found out some pretty interesting things, and like I said, I don't trust the Judds at all. You won't either when you know what I do. It makes me mad just to think about it. I'll come around and tell you."

She wanted me to ask her what it was, but I didn't care to know. "Don't bother," I said. "But I wish you'd come around and help me make a baby quilt."

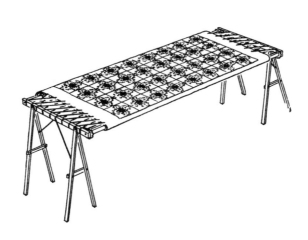

THE QUILT OF HAPPINESS

by Kate Douglas Wiggin

Oftentimes quilters pool their resources and
talents to make quilts for less fortunate members
of the community. In "The Quilt of Happiness,"
which appeared in the December 1917 issue of
the *Ladies' Home Journal*, Kate Douglas Wiggin
tells the story of Rebecca, a young, spirited girl
who gathers together a group of friends with
the purpose of making a quilt for Miss Roxy, an
elderly woman who lives alone in a house on
the outskirts of town. The girls work through
their holiday recess from school to deliver the
finished quilt in time for Christmas . . .com-
plete with a warm plate of food. Kate Douglas
Wiggin is the author of *Rebecca of Storybrook
Farm*, published in 1903.

School had been closed for two weeks now, and one
afternoon Rebecca leaned over her gate and surveyed the landscape. Emma Jane Perkins was
watching from her doorway, and Alice Robinson from
hers, while several other girls were concealed behind

board piles or clumps of trees, waiting for the hour of play to arrive. Suddenly all hearts leaped with gladness, for Rebecca was seen to remove the brown ribbon from one of her braids and put it in her apron pocket, and to substitute a piece of bright pink, legal tape.

"What are you doing to your hair, Rebecca?" asked Aunt Jane, coming to the door unexpectedly.

"Changing one of my ribbons, Aunt Jane."

"What for, child?"

"Well, it's a secret, Aunt Jane, but I don't mind telling you a bit: it's a signal. I can't fire a cannon or build a bonfire on the heights, so this is just a way of telling the girls I've got an idea."

"I should think they might guess that, any time, without your decking yourself out like a horse at a cattle fair," smiled Aunt Jane.

Rebecca laughed and shook her long braids. "But it's such a nice, ladylike, romantic way of signaling, Aunt Jane!"

"Well, maybe it is; but take it off before you come in the house, won't you?"

"As if I wouldn't, Aunt Jane? And, anyway, my idea is new, but it joins on to something you and Aunt Miranda know about already—Roxy's quilt."

"Oh!" sighed Miss Jane comfortably. "If it's nothing worse than that I won't worry."

"It's a beautiful idea!" and Rebecca glowed. "The girls will love it, and Miss Dearborn, and the minister's wife; and you would, too, but I mustn't show partiality between you and Aunt Miranda. The mothers will think it's silly, so it's got to be kept secret."

"I don't know. They all approved of your making extra patchwork, and if you're any happier to put your work together so that it will amount to something, and if you want to give it away, why, it's all to your credit, and it doesn't cost any one family much. You'd better give up the notion of quilting it, Rebecca."

"Oh, why, Aunt Jane?"

"Because you five girls could never finish it by cold weather. I'll put it in the frame for you and teach you how to 'tack' it."

"We all know how to quilt," objected Rebecca.

"Yes, but you don't know what it is to take those thousands of little stitches all in even rows. You can't break your thread, or make knots, or pucker the quilt; and the part near the edges of the frame is very hard to do neatly. Have you chosen your pattern?"

"No, we'll choose the pattern this afternoon. We've looked at all the spare bedroom quilts there are in Riverboro. There's Mrs. Perkins' 'Goose Chase' and Mrs. Robinson's 'Church Steps,' Mrs. Milliken's 'Rising Sun,' Mrs. Watson's 'Job's Troubles,' Mrs. Meserve's 'Duck's Foot in the Mud,' and—"

Miss Jane put her fingers in her ears. "Goodness gracious, Rebecca, how you do run on! I hope you don't forget your Aunt Miranda's 'Johnny Round the Corner'; but don't you girls fly too high or you'll come down heavy. You can get gay, pretty pieces and put four in a square and then join your squares corner to corner with plain ones in between. Perhaps Mrs. Perkins will have some new goods to help you out, and that'll set off the patchwork. Now, it's four o'clock and you can go and play, Rebecca."

REBECCA SPED LIKE AN ARROW shot from a bow. Emma Jane sped contemporaneously; Alice Robinson, Candace Milliken, and Persis Watson appeared as suddenly as if they had been concealed in woodchuck holes.

Miss Jane looked wistfully after the five slim little figures disappearing with arms about one another's waists and heads close together. "A child makes a wonderful difference," she thought. "I don't know what Aurelia's other children are like, but I can't think how she could part with Rebecca, even to get her educated! Anyhow it's put the sun back into the sky for me!"

Old Miss Roxanna Lyman lived half a mile up the river road and an eighth of a mile up a lane that led from it and stopped at her dooryard. Why the house was ever built there was a mystery. If you were a stranger in Riverboro and were walking up to play with the Simpson children and found everybody away from home, and had spied high-bush blueberries a little farther on, and chokecherry trees in full bearing in a green lane that you had never noticed before, and had strayed along the grass-grown road that had known hardly a wagon wheel for years, you would finally have passed an obscuring clump of trees and come suddenly upon Miss Roxy's little black house.

At least that was what Rebecca did. The door was open, and sitting in a rocking chair in the tiny entry was, as Rebecca reported to Miss Jane later, "the very most sorrowfulest old lady anyone had ever seen." No one could have told her age. She was slight and spare;

she was huddled in a gray shawl; the wrinkles in her face—wrinkles of pain, anxiety, grief, poverty, and foreboding—fairly made a latticework on the skin. You knew by looking at her that no one had gone out from the black house in the morning and no one was coming back to it at night.

Rebecca had heard of her and instantly asked: "Are you Miss Roxy Lyman? Please excuse me for stumbling right into your dooryard. I didn't see there was one till I was in it."

"Yes, I'm Roxy Lyman," said the old lady in a voice that trembled with surprise and suggested the rarity of callers. "Won't you set down a spell?"

Rebecca needed no second invitation to embark on a new experience. She sank down on the step, flung her hat on the grass, and pushed the hair back from her warm forehead. "I'm Rebecca Rowena Randall," she explained fluently. "My home is at Sunnybrook Farm, up Temperance way, but I'm living with my two Aunt Sawyers at the brick house so's to get educated. There's no education in Temperance, just plain teaching, and only a few months a year. Sometimes we didn't have any lessons at all, because when there were big boys it took all teacher's time to make them behave. Down here Miss Dearborn can manage a big boy as easy as anything, so of course we have nothing to do but learn."

This was only the natural beginning of a cataract of conversation, and the acquaintance between Rebecca and Miss Roxy Lyman was now well started. Rebecca proceeded to open her mind on a dozen subjects of passionate interest to herself. Clasping her knees with her hands she rippled on in a way never permitted at the brick house.

"I like the way your house is set," she said; "side end to the road, looking down over the fields and seeing the river flowing-ways. I think a black house with vines growing over it is nice too; a white one is always so stare-y. The river's splendid company, don't you think so?"

"It's all I have," was the reply. "I don't look at it much nowadays."

"I get tired of looking at the same old hat, but I never get used to the old river somehow; but perhaps it isn't quite enough company all by itself. Of course there's the trees."

"They ain't leaved out the year round," said Miss Roxy.

"No-o-o. But you're sure they *will* 'leave out.'" All this time Rebecca had stolen little side glances at Miss Roxy. "I suppose you read when you're not doing housework?" she ventured.

"I've read all my books over and over so I just set an' think!" And Miss Roxy's eyes wandered from Rebecca, as if she had already outlived the experience of meeting a new face and hearing a new voice.

"Well, all I was going to say is," said Rebecca, rising to her feet at this warning signal, "that there was a very sick lady, sick and lame and old, that lived half a mile from our farm, and mother always had me go over and tell her the news once or twice a week. Mother says everybody ought to know what's going on, or they get lonesome. I've come away from that lady so I think I'd better take you in her place if you'd like to have me. There's such a lot happens down our way—awfully interesting things too—that I could reel it off by the yard this minute, only you seem tired. And I've got two books of my own to lend you, so I'll come soon again if Aunt Miranda'll let me. Shall I?"

Rebecca's demeanor and tone were modest and innocent, but Miss Roxy felt herself in the grip of a master hand and feebly assented. "I don't mind if you do," she said, making an effort, and bringing her eyes back to the quaint, vivid little creature standing in front of her on the greensward. "Mebbe you'd liven me up."

"Oh, I would!" And Rebecca's tone was full of confidence. "Aunt Miranda says I'd stir up a cemetery; but that isn't a compliment. She doesn't like being stirred up; but I'd be real careful with you, being a stranger and not very well! Good-by!" And Rebecca flew down the lane, dark braids flying out behind her; while Miss Roxy, in spite of herself, rose to her feet by the rocking chair and watched the child out of sight.

There were many meetings after that. Sometimes Rebecca took one of the other girls and they carried a bouquet of wild flowers to put in a tumbler on the kitchen table, or some apples or berries or nuts that they had picked on the road; but it was easy to see that one caller at a time was all that Miss Roxy fancied. She had very little to eat and very little fuel, though she was known to receive ten dollars a month from a nephew in Salem, so that Riverboro was comfortably sure that she could not starve; and as for firewood, the same nephew had a load, all sawed and

split, deposited in her shed twice a year. These mer-
cies gave assurance of existence if not of luxury; and
anyway, Riverboro could not waste its time over an
incurably sad, cold, strange, silent woman like
Roxanna Lyman, even if her family had been one of
the best in former years.

Once Rebecca had knocked at Miss Roxy's door
without receiving any answer and, peeping into the
window of the downstairs chamber where she slept,
had seen her lying on her bed with the gray shawl
round her shoulders and a man's military coat over
her feet. Like lightning the thought flashed
through the child's mind: "Why not make a quilt
for Miss Roxy?"

Patchwork had to be sewed, day in and day out, as
was the custom. There were never enough sheets to
oversew, and needlework was a Christian duty; there-
fore, patchwork—in and out of season. It was cheap
too. Nobody would mind if she and the other girls did
extra work, begged their own pieces and gave away
the result for a Thanksgiving or Christmas present.
The matter had been put before mothers and aunts,
accepted, and scraps already collected. It only
remained to choose the design.

So far so good; but that was not why Rebecca had tied pink tape on one of her pigtails—not at all! The mere notion of the quilt, a secret from all the village save the families involved—this had enchanted the five girls from the beginning; but something else was unfolded in the pine grove meeting.

"You see," said Rebecca, "I was up to Miss Roxy's last night and she'd been crying. She cries 'most every day."

"What for, I wonder? She lives alone, so there's nobody to be cross to her," said Alice Robinson, who had troubles of her own.

"I guess it's the things that have happened in bygone days." (Rebecca had an incurably literary style in conducting meetings, and indulged unconsciously in flights of sentiment and rhetoric.) "Her mother and father died and her brother embezzled and Aunt Jane thinks that a gentleman played with her feelings and she's never been the same since."

"'Played with her feelings!' What's that?" inquired the unsentimental Emma Jane Perkins.

"Gave her hopes and then married another without saying so much as 'Boo,'" explained Rebecca.

"And there was a sister that did something dreadful, I don't exactly know what," hinted Candace darkly;

"but she lives out West and Miss Roxy writes and writes to her, but she never answers."

"And she was the one Miss Roxy loved best of all," added Rebecca with a tear in her voice. "I asked her yesterday why she didn't sit in the kitchen with a window open and not in the little front entry that'll hardly hold her rocking chair. She said if anybody should come any time suddenly she could get down the steps quicker to meet them. She never comes down to any of us, and I know it's the sister she means. Oh, dear!"

"Mother's awful sorry for her," was Persis's comment. "But everybody's kind of lost sympathy for her because she lives so out of creation, and it's so much work to get there."

"Well"—and Rebecca leaned toward the group confidentially—"I was thinking about it night before last as I was leaning over the gate. Now look the other way, girls, and don't laugh while I explain: All of a sudden I thought the pieces of our quilt will be scraps of dresses; why not take those that we, and all the other people, have had the loveliest times in? We could put them everywhere but round the edges, everywhere they'd touch Miss Roxy, I mean—on her neck and arms and waist and knees. It'd be a quilt of happiness then; that's my idea!" And Rebecca waited with flushing cheeks and downcast eyes for the verdict.

There was a breathless pause of half a minute. Emma Jane seldom moved her mind in the presence of Rebecca, feeling that competition was impossible; still she was the first to break the silence with her customary ejaculation: "I think that would be perfectly elegant!"

Alice Robinson nodded her curly head respon-sively and said: "'Quilt of Happiness!' It sounds lovely if we don't have to tell anybody grown up who would say it's silly."

"But can happiness strike *into* anybody?" inquired Candace, who, as the daughter of an Orthodox deacon, went to the foundation of things.

Rebecca was inclined to evade the direct ques-tion, inasmuch as her cherished idea had no real basis save one of pure sentiment. "I can't help feeling that if we just collect scraps of happiness," she said shyly, "and cut and stitch and tack happiness into the quilt, all in secret, that Miss Roxy'd feel warmer in it, though, of course, she'd never guess why."

"Well," answered Candace, unconvinced but gener-ously approving, "I think it couldn't do any harm to try."

"And there's just one person we might tell, for she'd understand and help us get the right pieces without telling our secret, and that's teacher." This suggestion from Persis Watson.

Rebecca clapped her hands delightedly. "Now here comes the greatest piece of news, and I've been saving it up till the end! I did tell Miss Dearborn, last evening. I couldn't help it, because I couldn't be sure my idea wasn't foolish till one other person had heard it—and what do you think she told me? She's engaged to be married! Miss Dearborn's engaged to be married!" This was chanted joyously while Rebecca skipped over the pine-needle carpet in circles and waved her arms triumphantly.

A chorus of "Oh!" and "Ah!" and "Who to?" woke the echoes.

Rebecca sat down again cross-legged and proceeded to the telling of a tale which from the beginning of the world has evoked the keenest joy in the narrator and the most rapt attention from the audience.

"How did she happen to tell you first?" asked Persis with a spice of envy in her tone.

"Just because I was there almost at the very identical minute when He went away."

"Who? Her beau?" inquired Alice, blushing to the roots of her hair.

"Yes; and she'd never tell Mrs. Bangs a thing like *that!*" (Mrs. Bangs was a lady of difficult temper with whom Miss Dearborn boarded as painlessly as possible.) "Don't you know how you feel when you're full to bursting with splendid news? That's how Miss Dearborn was. Do you remember the tall gentleman that came from Hartford two Saturday nights and went to meeting with her next day?"

"Yes!" in chorus. "Was that him?" (Miss Dearborn spoke and taught good English; but there are just some things that human beings are powerless to teach—or learn!)

"Yes. His name is Robert Hunt, and teacher says he's an ab-so-lute-ly glorious man!"

"I didn't know there was any glorious men," said Persis. "I wisht I'd looked at him harder in meetin'. When they goin' to be married?"

"Not till next summer, though he's pleaded for an early date (that's what she said). She wants to teach here till the spring term's over so's to buy her wedding clothes, and aren't you glad we'll have her one more winter? Now, why doesn't somebody ask me what my news is?"

"Gracious! Is there any more?" they cried.

"Of course! Or what has all this to do with our quilt? Miss Dearborn just loved the idea of its being a quilt of happiness. She kissed me lots of times, and then she got up and looked in the glass and twirled herself round and held up her skirt and danced, and she had on the dress we like best—the pink delaine with the moss rosebuds on it—and she said, thinking it out as she went along: 'Rebecca, I've had so much happiness today I must give part of it away! When Mr. Hunt asked me to marry him this afternoon I had on this dress. The waist is nearly worn out but the skirt is as good as new. It's got six breadths in it, and it'll make a beautiful lining for Miss Roxy's quilt!' Then I said: 'Oh, that'll be lovely if you can spare it; but, darling Miss Dearborn—excuse me for speaking of it—they say that long ago a gentleman from Boston played with Miss Roxy's feelings and that's partly the reason she's so unhappy, and oughtn't you to be perfectly sure that Mr. Hunt isn't playing with yours before you give away any clothes?'"

"That was very thoughtful of you, Rebecca," commented Persis approvingly. "And what did she say?"

"Oh! She fell into her rocking-chair and laughed and laughed till the tears rolled down her checks. Then she stood up and took the dress right off her back and kissed the waist of it and—"

EMMA JANE'S CHINA-BLUE EYES were popping out of her head. Her mind was hurrying to keep up with Rebecca's tale, but it seemed half a league behind as she ejaculated: "Kissed her waist? Wha' for?"

Rebecca looked embarrassed, both at the interruption at the high-water mark of her story and at the lack of comprehension. Also, it was a difficult action to explain in words; one whose meaning was to be felt with a blush and a heartbeat, but not dragged into the open and enlarged upon in bald speech.

"Just think it over, Emma Jane, for I can't talk about it," she said. "If you'd only read 'Ivanhoe,' as I wanted you to, or even 'Cora, the Doctor's Wife' or 'The Pearl of Orr's Island,' you'd know lots more about things."

"I know!" cried Candace triumphantly. "She'd had on the dress when he asked her to marry him, and she loved it."

"I can see how she'd kiss him, but I'd never 'a' thought of her kissin' a waist!" murmured Emma Jane obstinately.

"Well, she did!" Rebecca went on with heightened color. "She kissed it more'n twenty times as quick as lightning and hung it up in the closet, and then she laughed and cried some more and said: 'Oh, Rebecca, if you only knew how sure I am that Mr. Hunt isn't playing with my feelings; but I must tell him about your warning! Here, dear,' she said, rolling the skirt into a bundle, 'you'll have to piece the breadths to make them long enough, but featherstitching will cover the seams and, oh! I want to give it away right now when it's just warm with gladness and let it go to poor Miss Roxy, who hasn't got a splendid man to love her and take care of her like my Robert!'—that's what she called him." Rebecca's voice broke; her eyes glistened; her cheeks glowed.

Indeed, the little group of budding womanhood all felt vague thumpings and stirrings of something on the left side that had heretofore been silent. "Well, I declare!" "How perfectly elegant!" "Isn't it sweet of her!" "And now we've got our lining that's worried us the most." "And it's just fallen from heaven like the manna in the Bible!"

"And how wonderful to have a happiness lining all ready to put in our happiness quilt, the first happiness quilt that ever was! It simply must make a little difference in Miss Roxy's feelings!"

"And to think that we're the only ones in Riverboro to know that teacher's engaged to be married! It'll be all over the village tomorrow, and we knew it first! Oh, Rebecca, it's been the most wonderful meeting we've ever had, and when we see a pink tape on your pigtail again we'll run harder than ever!"

These and a dozen other excited comments fell from the girls' lips as they made their way home from the pine-grove meeting.

The collecting of the happiness pieces did not turn out to be a task of insuperable difficulty. The children themselves furnished a goodly number. There were some scraps of Rebecca's pink gingham, her first dress of the color she adored but had never hitherto possessed, having worn out her sister Hannah's clothes ever since she was born. Emma Jane gave bits of her Scotch-plaid poplin, called the hand-somest dress ever worn in Riverboro's younger set.

There were squares from frocks in which Persis and Candace had received school prizes and Alice Robinson had worn in tableaux. Alice was always in tableaux on account of her pink-and-white skin and golden hair, and was always cast for "the angel," although she had a most uncertain disposition.

The minister's wife, confidentially consulted, had contributed the full sleeves and shoulder cape of the dress she "appeared bride in" the Sunday after her wedding. "I had to walk up the aisle and sit in my pew all alone that summer, Rebecca, and I was only seventeen," she said. "Sometimes I thought it would be nice to be married to just a man that belonged to me only, and have him sit beside me in meeting; but then I remembered how grateful I ought to be that my husband belonged to God."

Aunt Jane gave two squares of the cherry-colored glacé silk that she wore when she danced with the governor of Maine at an inauguration ball at Augusta.

Aunt Miranda never knew that the quilt had any sentimental notions worked into it, or she would have thrown cold water on the entire proposition; but in her ignorance she looked over her piece-bag one rainy afternoon with Rebecca. Suddenly she chanced upon a bit of dun-colored stuff that resembled haircloth in texture.

"There!" she exclaimed. "That was the best dress I ever had! It wore me like iron! I put two braids on the bottom of it the fourth year and new under-arm pieces the next spring, and I believe it lasted me nine seasons. I never had so much comfort out of anything as that dress! It's a pleasure to look back upon!"

"Did you look nice in it, Aunt Miranda?" Rebecca inquired with interest.

"I don't know's I ever noticed," her aunt replied absentmindedly. "I know it covered me up, an' that's what dresses are for, I guess."

"Can I have a piece of it as well as of your gray cashmere?" asked Rebecca; and as she put it in her sewing basket she thought: "I wonder if Aunt Miranda never came any closer to happiness than that!"

I am afraid that from an artistic standpoint the quilt of happiness was not a very handsome one. The idea having been the most important thing in the working out of the design, every conceivable manner of stuff had been employed—calico, gingham, silk, poplin, percale, organdie, Henrietta cloth, delaine, velveteen, challie, and cashmere; but the squares had been combined with such loving care that the effect was gay and attractive, if a little bizarre.

At any rate, the very angels themselves might have been pleased to look down on the five bright heads—yellow, chestnut, auburn, and brown—that bent every day over their self-imposed task!

There were five lame middle fingers aching from the pressure of brass thimbles, and five forefingers pricked with needle marks, but there were no complaints.

Rebecca's energy flagged now and then, for long and monotonous tasks were not her strong point; and, if it had not been a quilt of happiness, her share in it might never have been accomplished. It was just a little girl's dream—rainbow-tinted, fanciful, baseless; but it danced in and out of the patchwork squares like a vagrant summer breeze, and somehow it danced through the heart, too, ripening and sweetening it.

And at last, in late November, there came a day of days when, in an empty chamber at Emma Jane's house (Miranda Sawyer had refused to have the girls bringing in dirt and carrying it up and down the stairs of the brick house), Mrs. Perkins and Aunt Jane stretched the quilt into its frame, suspended on the backs of four wooden chairs. Miss Dearborn, who grew prettier every day and came from the post office in the afternoons all smiles and beams and dimples, had made the happiness lining herself and featherstitched the seams.

Mrs. Perkins, whose father had been a storekeeper, leaving her enormous riches in the shape of new goods, brought from her attic her contribution of rolls of sheet wadding.

Now the outside, the wadding, and the lining were held carefully in place by hands that were moist with excitement and responsibility, and the tacking of the three smoothly together with bright colored worsteds proved to be the most difficult task that the girls had yet confronted.

There was a week's work in all this, and two or three afternoons when the binding of the four long sides was done; but, by dint of perseverance, the last stitch was put into the quilt on the day before Christmas, when Aunt Jane had prophesied New Year's as the nearest possible date of completion. The girls gazed at their work with uncontrollable admiration and reverence.

"I'm sick to death of it!" exclaimed Rebecca. "I love it to distraction, and I never want to see another as long as I live! How can anybody make 'em for fun? I could hug it, I'm so fond of it, and slap it, I'm so tired of it!" And the girls echoed her sentiments, though in less picturesque and vigorous language.

"If we give it to her today, she'll have something to be thankful for on Christmas Day," the girls decided. "We'll have to lug it up together, and let Rebecca go in with it while we stay out in the road and wait."

"Don't say 'lug,' and let's go after dark," Rebecca suggested. "I believe I can open the door and put it down softly in the entry with our letter; then I won't get thanked all by myself, which wouldn't be fair; and we can take turns going up tomorrow to hear what she says."

"Mother's going to send her a big plate of dinner," said Alice.

"Oh, joy!" And Rebecca took out the pink tape from her apron pocket and tied it on a pigtail.

"What is it?" the girls asked breathlessly in chorus.

"Why, once there was a very important paper that had to be sent to a certain king by one of his generals, and he stationed messengers ten miles apart all along the road from his camp to the king's palace. One man galloped for ten miles, got off his hot, steaming charger, and handed the message to another man, who was all ready and waiting on a fresh horse. He galloped on to the next man, and so on. We'll do the same with Miss Roxy's dinner, each of us making believe it's horseback, and running like mad to give the basket to the next one. Then it'll get there piping hot!"

CHRISTMAS EVE FELL COLD AND BLEAK, with a north wind and an uncertain moon. The girls put on mittens and hoods and, starting at six o'clock, when it was quite dark, they carried the quilt as they walked, Indian file, along the frozen road. They met no one, just as they had planned, for as the affair had begun in secrecy, so it was hoped to end it. That was half the fun.

The Simpson cottage, with its yard completely filled with ramshackle vehicles and cast-off implements of every sort, was lighted by the effulgence of the tall banquet lamp that Rebecca and Emma Jane had earned as a premium for selling soap. It was the joy and pride of the Simpsons, although as drawing-room furniture it was accompanied only by a battered pine table and three rickety wooden chairs.

The girls admired its glow in passing, but kept on the dark side of the road and went stealthily by to avoid being hailed by Clara Belle Simpson. Midway up the lane four of them stayed behind a clump of young pines while Rebecca went on alone, staggering under the weight of the precious quilt.

It was cold and the teeth of the "waiters" chattered, but by dint of walking 'round and 'round the trees they succeeded in keeping fairly comfortable, as their blood was circulating with incredible rapidity and they were palpitating with excitement.

Soon Rebecca came running lightly down the lane. "Wait till we get into the road," she whispered, "and I'll tell you all, though everything went just right. Now come close and keep walking. I looked through the kitchen window and saw a lamp burning on the table, but nobody there. Then I opened the front door softly and went in on tiptoe, thinking Miss Roxy was upstairs or down cellar, and that I'd put the quilt on a chair with our letter. But the door was open into the kitchen chamber and I could see her there asleep. She hadn't gone to bed for good, I guess, because she wasn't undressed. She was lying there with her gray shawl and a black jacket over her shoulders, and her father's soldier coat over her feet. Then I had an idea!"

"Of course!" they laughed in chorus.

"So I crept in like a mouse, lifted off the coat and jacket very softly, and spread the quilt over her!"

Here Rebecca's emotion quite overcame her. She stopped still in the road and clasped her hands dramatically, while the girls listened with devouring eagerness.

"Oh!" she said under her breath. "If only you had all been there! The quilt was beautiful beyond compare! Miss Roxy looked like a queen in it, spread all over everything—so big, so thick, so rich and bright! Her face was as white as her hair, and her eyes were shut tight. I tiptoed out, so afraid she'd wake up and have to thank me. But it seemed to me I must go back once, to see if she had moved, and take one last look; so I crept round to the back and peeped in the window. Just then she put out her hand and I thought she'd feel something strange and open her eyes, but she didn't. She just pulled it up round her neck; then she snuggled down into it the way you do when you know you're going to sleep that instant minute and have a lovely dream. And then the moon came out and shone on her face, so I can't be perfectly certain, though I was looking hard, but I think, I really do think, that she smiled."

Here Rebecca stopped suddenly, turned her head away, and swallowed a lump that appeared unexpectedly in her throat.

Emma Jane, who adored her, pressed her arm fondly but uncomprehendingly. "You are the queerest!" she exclaimed. "I never saw anybody before who cried when she was pleased!"

Rebecca, all smiles again, dashed away the coming tear. "I've told you before, Emma Jane," she said, "that you'd know lots of things if only you'd read books. 'Cora, the Doctor's Wife' and 'The Pearl of Orr's Island' always cried when they were happy. I feel as if laughs and cries came out of the same spot inside of me!"

Rebecca was right and the moon told the truth. Miss Roxy had smiled, and she had dreamed. Dreams were rare occurrences in her experience, for her nights were as drab and colorless as her days. The dream carried her so far into the past that she was a child again; and the something warm that she felt about her neck was her sister's arm—the sister she loved best of all.